ANGELS WATCHING OVER ME

ANGELS WATCHING OVER ME

BETTY MALZ

Published by

chosen books

FLEMING H. REVELL COMPANY
OLD TAPPAN, NEW JERSEY

Library of Congress Cataloging in Publication Data

Malz, Betty.
  Angels watching over me.

  1. Angels. 2. Christian life—1960– . I. Title.
BT966.2.M35   1986   235'.3   85-26322
ISBN 0-8007-9056-1

Edited by Ann McMath
Designed by Ann Cherryman

A Chosen Book
Copyright © 1986 by Fleming H. Revell Company
Chosen Books are Published by
Fleming H. Revell Company
Old Tappan, New Jersey
Printed in the United States of America

*This book is dedicated to bringing hope
to the helpless
and offering help
to the fearful*

CONTENTS

ACKNOWLEDGMENTS

My appreciation to:
  Ann McMath for her editorial advice
  Len LeSourd who challenged me to take this
    assignment
  P.J. Zondervan who believed that I could do it
  My friend Vicky Hagen for her prayer support
and to:
  Dwight Fearing
  Delores Eggen
  Gloria Hutchens
  Sheri Knipe
  Dr. Donald Van Hoozier
  Veva Rose
  Dr. Marvin Perkins, my brother
  Clarinne Koeppe
  Carl Nelson
  Patty Opsal
  John Pryor and Mark Torness
  Rev. Millington from England
for their input, research, and suggestions.

INTRODUCTION

I once commented to our old missionary friend Morris Plotts, "I'd like to read a good book on working angels."

"Why don't you write one then?" he said simply.

"Not me," I protested. I was hesitant about tackling such a big subject, though angels held a fascination for me. Plus, my practical nature did not want me to be classified with people who mount angels on their automobiles for hood ornaments and boast of private angel-servants on command.

He pressed the point. "Read the 'future' book," he said, "the prophetic book of things to come, Revelation. It mentions angels all the way through, who in the last days will govern the affairs of men and nations, control the weather and war, fight battles, declare the Gospel of Jesus, and announce His coming back to the earth again. More and more," he added thoughtfully, "as we draw closer to that day, angels are helping God's servants reach the ends of the earth with the Gospel."

I agreed it all sounded like a fascinating study, and later I wondered if he was really right about angels' increased activity in this world. Mostly, it seems, we are not even aware of them, or else we remember them only as celestial beings who heralded important events in Bible times.

I tried to put the suggestion aside but, curiously, it seemed to pursue me, and I came to realize he *was* right. Whenever I traveled on a speaking tour, whether being interviewed before a nationwide television audience or talking with a fellow airline passenger, someone would excitedly confide his own angel story. My friend Morris was not without one, either, perhaps the most fascinating I have ever heard. Even television commercials seemed to jump out at me with the clever use of angel characters.

And I discovered that the more I pondered the angel book, the more I felt driven to write about the encouragement evident in their activities. I wanted to write a comforting book that would stimulate ordinary people to tap the extraordinary resources of angelic assistance. I became utterly convinced that God uses angels to help us through the impossible places of life, times we cannot make it unless He helps us.

This book, then, is a practical journey of adventure. It is not meant to entertain, but to search out the ways angels work, the specific times they help us, and how we can have the right perspective about them. Some of the stories will sound almost incredible, but then, no more so than biblical accounts of angels at work.

It was a fascinating search, one that actually began years ago with my own encounter with an angel—my guardian angel. Perhaps my story is not typical in that I am alive to tell about it, for amazingly enough, I had to die to begin to understand the significant role angels play in our lives.

But now I'm getting ahead of myself.

Swing low, sweet chariot,
Comin' for to carry me home.
Swing low, sweet chariot,
Comin' for to carry me home.
    All night, all day,
    Angels watchin' over me, my Lord.
    All night, all day,
    Angels watchin' over me.

(From "Swing Low, Sweet Chariot")

1

BETWEEN
TWO WORLDS

When we left for vacation that spring of 1959 I had no idea how my life was about to change. My husband, daughter, and I were traveling with my parents to sunny Florida, and other than a nagging uneasiness, which I chose to ignore, my life could not have been better.

I attributed my security to my very practical faith—I had given my heart to Jesus as a child and knew I would go to heaven when I died—and I felt satisfied at my refusal to believe anything I could not see or explain. Since there was no earthly reason for me to feel apprehensive, I continued to shrug off a slight discomfort in my side that tugged for attention.

Then, suddenly one night, I passed the stage of warning. I felt as though something was exploding in my side, boiling and burning mercilessly. An ambulance rushed me to a hospital near our hotel.

Doctors struggled for days with a diagnosis until surgery revealed that I had suffered a ruptured appendix eleven days before, and that a mass of gangrene had coated all of my organs, causing them to disintegrate. Even as I lapsed into a coma I argued with the likelihood of such news, while my praying family thanked God that I had lived as long as I had. Out of my hearing, the doctors explained to my family that further complications of pneumonia and collapsed veins meant I could not live long.

Early one morning, after I had hung on in a coma for forty-four days, the night nurse on the third floor came to check my vital signs and found no response to her probings. I had slipped from this life into the next. At five a.m. a doctor pronounced me clinically dead, pulled a sheet over my head, and left the room in darkness. That was the state in which my father, who had awakened in the night with an urgent desire to be with me, found me twenty-eight minutes later.

I knew nothing of these earthly activities, of course. I felt as though I were on a roller coaster ride at Disneyland, and arrived at my destination when I reached the highest peak of exhilaration. It was much like taking the fastest jet imaginable from earth to another planet—a bright and glorious place under a deep blue sky. There was no fear, only peacefulness and beauty.

I was immediately aware of majestic music, filled with exquisite harmonies from countless choirs. Around my feet living waves of flowers splashed the velvet green meadows with color.

I felt fulfilled, youthful, alive as I walked tall and erect up a beautiful hill toward a brilliant city. I had never experienced such joy or eager anticipation.

Then I realized I was not alone. I glanced to my left and saw a tall companion in flowing white robes. An angel! I remembered childhood thoughts about angels, wondering what they did and what they looked like, but I could never have imagined a being with such beauty, power, and assurance. His face had masculine features; his hands were large and strong.

I felt comfortable in his presence, and somehow knew that he had been with me from the time I was thirteen and asked Jesus to be my Lord and Savior. I had never known he was there, possibly because I had never been so aware of my surroundings—or my need. For, without a doubt, he was a necessary part of my transition from the life I was leaving to the new life just ahead.

Silently, side by side, we took long, even strides up the sloping hillside. We spoke no words, but communicated easily just by thinking what we wanted to express. I also realized we could travel as quickly as our thoughts could choose a destination. For instance, a desire to see my earthly grandmother of my childhood days could transport us to her porch swing with warm summer breezes and honeysuckle sweetening the air. Yet we walked steadily toward our mutual destination.

We reached an enormous sheet of translucent pearl, apparently a gate in the city walls, through which I could detect a great brightness. My guardian angel reached his hand out to touch it, and as if from the warmth of his touch, a hand-sized opening melted outward to the borders of the gate.

Instantly I was bathed in a warm light and felt completely whole. Every yearning of my heart found fulfillment in the flooding power of that light. Many times during shining moments of accomplishment in my life, there had remained a small cavity of emptiness in the secret chambers of my soul. I knew now that that had been the longing for this new home; nothing else could fill it.

My eyes were drawn to the One who sat on a golden throne, and I saw the source of the dazzling light. The face of Jesus glowed with a brilliance too bright to behold. I looked down. It reflected on the golden boulevard in the center of the city, and was the same light that flowed through me.

Others besides my companion and me were drawn by the power of that light. I recognized people around the throne who had died during my lifetime, and they knew me. We shared the knowledge that we had achieved our true identities, we had become what we had always yearned to be.

Many people were doing just what people do on earth, though without any hindrance or handicap. I watched as several florists busily tended some delicate flowers like the ones I had admired on the way up the hill. Yet here they were working for a different employer in a perfect setting—no drought, no bugs, no backaches. Likewise, builders were busy constructing dwellings (I knew somehow that they were expecting large numbers of people soon) and countless others pursued their dreams.

I thought I would never want to leave that awesome place, but that was to change. Looking to the right I watched as shafts of light, ascending directly from the earth, entered the throne room and the presence of the original great Light—the Source of all energy, warmth, creativity, and power. The shafts of light, straight and swift as laser beams, were prayers. And standing all around the throne room were armies of angels waiting for orders to execute the answers.

On a particular shaft, I saw as well as heard a one-word prayer, and I recognized the voice of the one praying. It was my father. He simply breathed the name *Jesus,* and in it was a wish that I had not died. His prayer became my desire.

Immediately I felt as though I were on a fast elevator, descending at an alarming speed. Then I slowed down and stopped. All was still. I opened my eyes in my hospital room and looked into my dad's astonished face. I had returned to life.

The doctor who had declared me dead was shocked. He validated that I had been dead for twenty-eight minutes, and sent me home two days later with no discernible physical difficulties from my extraordinary experience.

But I had learned invaluable lessons. I now have a better understanding of human relationships, for instance, and feel an overwhelming desire to tell others about Jesus. I also learned that I must not believe only what I can explain with my practical logic. And I realized that next to the ultimately fulfilling presence of God, what amazed me most were the activities of His ministering angels, beings I had never seen or bothered much about, although I had pleasant childhood associations with the idea of angels.

As early as I can remember, a painting entitled "Guardian Angel" hung in my grandparents' home. It showed a little boy and girl on a bridge that spanned a waterfall. The boy was picking wild flowers, leaning over several missing planks in the bridge, while his little sister was holding the flowers he had already picked. Perhaps they were picking them for a sick grandmother, or to surprise their parents at home. In any event, the message that came through to me at an early age was that the large angel behind them was assigned to protect them, especially since they were picking the flowers for someone else.

One night during a terrible storm I snuggled close to my grandmother and hid my face so I couldn't see the lightning and hear the deafening claps of thunder. Mom Burns reached for her flashlight, shone the beam on the guardian angel picture, and quoted Psalm 91:11. "For he shall give his angels charge over thee, to keep thee in all thy ways" (KJV).

Somehow the painting helped me picture what the Bible verse meant. The children were in a dangerous situation, but they were being "kept in all their ways." Thinking about God's angels protecting me, too, in a dangerous situation helped me not be afraid.

Twenty-two years later that lesson of angelic protection was driven home. My six-year-old daughter, Brenda, and I were home alone, praying for safety as a tornado destroyed dozens of houses around us. I pointed to the guardian angel picture, which now hung in our living room, and spoke aloud the verse from Psalm 91.

Within seconds, our house was hit by the force of the tornado. Winds lifted the roof with a tremendous crack. Brenda and I huddled close in the corner. When we could finally uncover our faces and look around us, we saw that only one wall was left standing, while the two of us and Smokey, our small dog, were safe without a scratch.

Two miles away from where our house had stood I found some family photos, a light fixture, and the water-soaked guardian angel picture. It now is a treasured reminder of God's protection through his ministering angels. I knew for certain they were around us, helping us.

As a matter of fact, it seems I have survived a number of life-threatening situations, so many that I always remember with a smile the way. I was introduced at a Full Gospel Business Men's Convention in San Angelo, Texas. A big Texan put his arm around my shoulder and said to the audience, "This is Betty Malz. With all she has survived, you might say this cat has nine lives!" Everyone laughed, and I have since mused inwardly that God must have needed an extra crew of guardian angels for me, a well-meaning but often unwise young woman:

I was stillborn at birth, took poison once by mistake thinking it was medicine, and nearly married a mentally deranged man because he was good-looking and because I was deceived by my lonely heart. I survived a ruptured appendix, managed to veer my car at the last second from a gaping sinkhole in Florida, and lived through the tornado that destroyed our home in Indiana. I escaped from an overturned car in North Dakota, and almost crashed in a plane over Santa Ana, California.

Now that I have walked side-by-side with my angel and have seen countless other angels standing by the throne ready for instruction, I not only believe that angels exist—I have become increasingly fascinated with their activity here on earth. I know they are commissioned on our behalf—I watched them bolt like lightning to fulfill God's commands—but I began to be intrigued by a succession of questions. Do I have just one guardian angel? Or are there other angels available to intervene on my behalf? Just when can we human beings look for their help? When do they oversee ordinary, day-to-day activities? Is my angel always watching over me, by my side at every moment? I thought I knew the answer to that last question. I believed he was always with me; yet there was something significant about his presence in that experience of walking through death that only led to more questions about angels' help in our lives.

Was there some common denominator in these and other experiences that might explain when angels are available to help?

In all of the stories of angels that I ran across I did find a common denominator—aside from their willingness to help: all the people angels assisted seemed to be caught in some kind of gap. By that I mean they had a need they were powerless to meet. Perhaps they lacked the strength or knowledge or physical stamina to change a situation. During my near-death experience, for instance, I was helped by an angel in a gap between two worlds.

Just as God sought someone in Old Testament times to "stand in the gap" for Israel through intercession (see Ezekiel 22:30), so we are sometimes called to stand in a gap, whether of intercession or action. The personal experiences I encountered fell into five specific gap situations. You may be as surprised as I was to find that we are in these gaps far more than we realize. What a comfort to know that the Lord's hosts are *always* watching over us!

2

WHEN DO ANGELS COME?

My minister father almost regretted opening our rural community's Wednesday prayer meeting one night with this question: "Does anyone have an answer to prayer you would like to tell us about before we take prayer requests?"

Several hands went up, and my father nodded to a man sitting in the row behind me. I was a child, but even to me Clyde seemed a frail little man, unlike his rotund wife Samantha. Standing, his hat in his hands, Clyde told us his story.

"I was tryin' to sleep last night, but there were a mouse in our closet that jest kep' gnawin' and makin' a racket. So I prayed and told God to send an angel to kill that pesky mouse fer me.

"Shore 'nuff," Clyde continued, "this mornin' right by the closet door, there it were. Flat as a pancake."

From the look of polite consternation on my father's face, I knew he must have been groping for a spiritual conclusion. Before he could think up one, Samantha, who was seated directly behind me, rolled forward and stood up. I knew from experience that whenever she sat behind me and rose to her feet, her enormous stomach would bounce my head forward. So I slid to the edge of my pew and turned to look at her with what I hoped, under my parents' watchful eyes, was respectful interest.

"Folks," she said with a big smile, "I cain't let this go by. That weren't no angel that killed that mouse. 'Twere me, myself. I took Clyde's house slipper and smashed it." She heaved herself down in her pew, whereupon Clyde popped up once more.

"That's okay," he said, nodding to the smiling faces turned up at him. "It jest goes to show that God can use any old thing to he'p His angels answer your prayin'."

My father had apparently collected his thoughts by that time, and responded good-naturedly, but I hardly heard, my attention was so captivated by Clyde's face. I'll never forget his satisfied look as he explained the wonders of God's angels as he saw them.

As I thought of that humorous episode years later, I agreed that God can indeed use "any old thing" to work out His plans for good, though perhaps we should be more selective in what jobs we expect angels to perform!

Somehow I doubted that angels would be dispatched for work we could easily handle ourselves, or for foolish fancy. But I wondered. . . . If there are certain times we know angels *won't* come, are there guaranteed times they *will* come? What kinds of distresses must we be facing before they will act on our behalf? If we knew more about their ministry, perhaps we could understand when to look for them. Just what was a proper understanding of the role of angels in our lives?

The Bible seemed the best place to find an answer. And even a quick look through my concordance left me amazed at the many accounts of angels in Scripture.

An angel helped Abraham's servant choose a wife for Isaac (Genesis 24:7).

Jacob saw angels ascending and descending a heavenly ladder as they received and delivered communications and executed God's desires for His children (Genesis 28:12).

Moses received instructions through the angel of the Lord in the burning bush (Exodus 3:2).

While Balaam was planning to curse the children of God for personal profit, there stood in the path before him, though he could not detect it, an angel of the Lord. The mule saw it, however, and would not trot past the angelic roadblock. This saved the lives of many Israelites, including Balaam himself (Numbers 22:32–33).

Angels announced not only Jesus' birth but also His resurrection (Luke 1–2; Matthew 28:5–7); and they will be with Jesus when He comes again (Matthew 24:30–31; 1 Thessalonians 4:16).

An angel visited Paul, giving him assurance that later saved 276 souls from shipwreck (Acts 27:22–24).

An angel visited the house of Cornelius at three o'clock one afternoon and told him that God had heard his many prayers and seen what he had done for the people. Because of this visit, Cornelius' household was saved (Acts 10:2–3).

An angel of the Lord directed Philip in his ministry (Acts 8:26–40).

Angels rejoice over sinners who repent (Luke 15:10) and are witnesses when Jesus declares us to be His followers (Luke 12:8).

As followers of Jesus—the King of Angels as a hymn declares—we look to Him as the supreme example of the Christian life. And from the number of accounts recorded in the Bible of Jesus' alliance with angels, I concluded they must be an impor-tant—even vital—part of God's dealings with His earthly children.

Almost everyone is familiar with the stories of angels surrounding Jesus' birth—how they brought the news to Mary, Joseph, the shepherds in the fields. But what about His life as an adult? What connection did He have then with angels?

In the Gospel of Matthew, Jesus first appeared publicly at His baptism in the Jordan River. Immediately afterward, we are told in chapter four, the Holy Spirit led Him into the wilderness where He fasted and was tempted by the devil. After He had rejected the devil's temptation, we read: "Then the devil left him, and angels came and attended him" (verse 11). Jesus needed strength for a spiritual battle against a relentless enemy. He was hungry and physically weak, and angels came and ministered to Him, giving Him just what He needed.

Suppose you and I have also been fighting spiritual battles, trying to change our world for the better. Should we expect angels to minister to us with supernatural power? That seems almost too good to be true!

Jesus lived a perfect life. He obeyed the Father in all things. It seems absolutely right that He should have heavenly assistance. But remember that He is our example. I cannot live a perfect life, but I can try to do my best to be like Him. First Peter 1:15 says that "just as he who called you is holy, so be holy in all you do." Could it be that my struggle to "grow up into him who is the Head" (Ephesians 4:15), to follow His example, includes an expectant belief, as He Himself had, in angelic help?

I couldn't help but wonder about other men and women of faith in the Bible, and I found almost invariably that God's servants were ministered to in difficult situations by angels.

When Elijah, for instance, went to Mount Carmel to prove to the Baal worshipers that there was only one true God, he was helpless to convince them on his own (see 1 Kings 18:21). Elijah had challenged fifty false prophets to a test. They would each prepare a sacrificial offering. Then the followers of Baal were to call on their god to send fire to consume their offering, and Elijah would pray to his

God to light the other. Whoever answered with fire from heaven would be acknowledged as the true God.

Elijah could not have brought fire down from the sky any more than the Baal worshipers could, but he trusted God to act. After the pagans' failure to light the offering, to further prove it was God at work, Elijah doused the slain bull and the wood around it with water three times.

Then he looked up to heaven and prayed: "O Lord, God of Abraham, Isaac and Israel, let it be known today that you are God in Israel and that I am your servant and have done all these things at your command. Answer me, O Lord, answer me, so these people will know that you, O Lord, are God, and that you are turning their hearts back again" (1 Kings 18:36–37).

I like to imagine scores of angels with fiery torches gathering at the gate of heaven, receiving the command, "Go!" The fire poured out of heaven.

When the offering was consumed with flames that licked up even the water in the surrounding trench, Elijah killed the fifty false prophets and won quite a few converts to the true God.

His experience of angelic assistance came not long after. When Elijah heard that the wicked Queen Jezebel intended to avenge the blood of her slain prophets on him, he fled into the wilderness and hid under a tree. Apparently fear had caused him to forget that when we are serving God, He keeps us in His protective care. After telling the Lord how weary and discouraged he was, he slept.

But Elijah had never moved out from under the Lord's protection. He had been obedient and the Lord did not forget him. An angel appeared with nourishment and jostled Elijah awake: "Arise, and eat." Elijah was fed cake and water in a parched and dry land, and went for forty days on the strength of that one heaven-sent meal.

This account of the Old Testament prophet gives us at least three important directives for expecting angelic assistance. First, *Be obedient*. If we enter an impossible situation through the Lord's leading, we can expect His hosts to defend us. Second, *Be selfless*. If we are promoting a self-serving cause we have no right to look for helpful divine intervention. But if we are doing what God calls us to do, out of a motive of love and service to others, we can and should expect special treatment. And third, *Honor God*. This may be the most important principle of all. Aren't we supposed to love the Lord God with all our heart, soul, mind, and strength?

About the time I was first absorbing these angelic lessons from Elijah, I was also preparing to speak at the Minneapolis Convention Center at a Lowell Lundstrom Ministries Camp Meeting. In the weeks before the convention, my husband and I had attended to our daughter's graduation, tried to sell our farm, packed and moved to North Dakota, and hosted a seven-day reunion with fifteen people in our new home. On top of that, I had had a root canal, an abscess, an infection in my bladder, and leg cramps.

On the July day I was to speak, the humidity in

Minnesota measured ninety-two percent. I was just about to cancel out—I could not endure it physically—when I recalled how angels had ministered to Jesus and Elijah. I remembered the words from Scripture, "Ye ask and receive not because ye ask amiss" (James 4:3, KJV). And I couldn't escape the conviction that He wanted me to speak at the Convention Center that night. So, I decided to ask Him for angelic help.

Hours later, exhausted but obedient, I stepped up to the podium, and certain words of the Apostle Paul's came to mind. I smiled and spoke a variation of them into the microphone: "I, Betty, come not to you with enticing words, but with a toothache, a leg ache, a bladder infection, and runs in my stockings."

We all laughed, and I felt new strength. I was there to help minister to the needs of people, and like Jesus, my example, I would pray for them.

Then, at the very moment I vowed inwardly to stand firm and believe that God would meet my needs in order for me to serve Him, I felt a pulsating sensation all over my body, even in my scalp. As the current-like force passed through me, the aches and pains left, and we enjoyed a glorious evening together.

Now, I can't report that I saw an angel doctor with a medical bag, or that everyone in the audience observed a glowing nimbus over my head. But I can say that Jesus sends provisions on the wings of angels, and that I am still going on the strength of that answered prayer. Like Elijah, I was exhausted until I tapped His energy. What joy I felt at Jesus' desire to send those throne-room angels here to help us.

My enthusiasm was almost short-circuited a few days later when a woman named LoRae came to me with a troubling question. She was a young mother whose twenty-eight-year-old husband, a pilot, had died in a plane crash. We talked about Bill's death, until this young widow's voice burst out angrily: "Where was Bill's guardian angel when he crashed into that bridge? My relatives are religious people and told me he is safe in the arms of Jesus because he was a believer. But that's not much comfort. My in-laws say it was predestined— what is to be will be and cannot be diverted—and they told me to change my bitterness to relinquishment. But that just leaves me with more questions. Why pray for safety? Why pray at all?"

When I didn't answer right away, LoRae repeated her unresolved question: "Why didn't an angel protect Bill?"

I could not think of a satisfying answer, but I could pray for one. So we bowed our heads and I prayed for her comfort, asking God to heal her grief. Then I asked God to speak to her personally. We are all the same distance, after all, from the throne room of God; we can all enter it by prayer. She seemed more peaceful after we prayed, and I hoped that soon we would both know the answer to her question.

Months later, I learned how LoRae's grief did lift. She married a fine young man whose wife had died from a heart condition. She found happiness. And in a telephone conversation one day, as LoRae reminisced about her first husband, I stumbled upon what seemed to be the answer to her question.

He had been nicknamed "Wild Bill" for the foolhardy chances he sometimes took while flying. He was most cautious in his business flights, or when his family flew with him, but when alone he seemed to revel in danger. He had been warned by the county sheriff that another infraction of the law, such as flying lower than the five-thousand-foot ceiling, would cost him his license. The day of the crash, two motorists had stopped to report to the police a pilot "buzzing" cars on the highway below, and diving over and under power lines. Bill even flew low and close enough to talk by radio with truckers on their CB's.

Suddenly all seemed clear. I had just been reading a variety of Scripture passages that had to do with God's caring love. They made it clear that no one can pluck us out of the hollow of His hand; that He keeps us as the apple of His eye; that He protects us under the shadow of His wing. In other words, He will never *dump* us out of the hollow of His hand, but we can carelessly *jump* out. Paul writes in the first few verses of Romans 13 that "everyone must submit to the governing authorities. Do what is right and he (the one in charge) will commend you. For he is God's servant to do you good."

LoRae finally saw as well as I did that it was possible to violate the laws of government, of nature, of any established authority, and move out of the "safety zone" in which angels will protect us. Bill's choice to break federal aviation laws removed him from the sphere of angelic protection. He put his survival in his own hands, and took one too many chances.

I do not feel that the perimeters of angelic protection are so fragile that we should fear making one false move and losing that help forever. But I do believe that, so long as man's laws accord with God's laws, He expects us to follow their conditions and limitations. Choosing to disobey them does block angelic assistance just as surely as unbelief limits God's work in our lives.

Does this mean we will have no hardships? I think not. Our church congregation used to sing these lines from an old hymn: "Must Jesus bear the cross alone and all the world go free? No, there's a cross for everyone, and there's a cross for me." We must be willing to go where Jesus leads us, for as He told His disciples, "If anyone would come after me, he must deny himself and take up his cross and follow me" (Matthew 16:24).

Paul spent a considerable amount of time in chains for preaching the Gospel, yet he was rescued and guided by angels as well. Peter must have remembered that Jesus told him, "Simon, Simon, Satan has asked to sift you as wheat. But I have prayed for you, Simon, that your faith may not fail. And when you have turned back, strengthen your brothers" (Luke 22:31–32). Did angels minister to Peter, fight on his behalf, and defend him until he turned, stronger than ever to serve his Lord? Did angels keep him in their care as he was tried sorely, until he was able to bear even death for his Lord? Yes!

Each of us may be called in turn to serve in different ways, but we know God will not let us be tempted beyond what we are able to bear (1 Corinthians 10:13). Our God is a good God who does not want us to suffer senseless tragedies.

But that thought may make us a little uneasy. As with Bill, it puts a certain responsibility on *us.* He is perfect and loving; He wants us to lay hold of His provisions. So why do we seem to fall so short of the mark? If we are trying to obey legitimate authority, live good, unselfish lives, and honor God, and if angels surround us, willing to protect us, then why do we so often find ourselves struggling helplessly?

Could it be that we fail to take advantage of our prerogative as believers to pray, actively pray, for angels to help us serve God?

After my conversation with LoRae, I thought of the verse that came to mind that hot July night at the convention when the Lord answered my prayer for strength: "Ye have not because ye ask not." I realized I had a lot to learn about this kind of praying, but the more I discovered stories of angels' appearances in answer to specific prayers, the more I felt assured this was indeed important.

One of these stories was relayed by a young father I met shortly before an appearance on a Christian television program.

Steve Doherty, who works for the Trinity Broad-

casting Network, told me of the struggle he
wife, Theresa, had once had getting their young son
to sleep peacefully through the night. I was especially interested in this problem since I get letters
and phone calls constantly from parents whose
children between the ages of four and nine are
afraid to go to sleep.

For two long years, every night from the time he
was four, Ryan Doherty would cry at bedtime, beg
to sleep with his parents, and wake up several times
in the night terrified from nightmares. Steve and
Theresa tried everything. They played Christian
music, read happy bedtime stories, reassured him,
prayed with him—even spanked him. They coun-
seled with a pediatrician and talked with a children's psychiatrist; and always, it seemed, they
were told that they had done everything they could
to assure Ryan he was safe and loved. They were
completely baffled.

Finally an elderly gentleman in their church
suggested they try two things. First, he said, when
Ryan went to bed, they should have him breathe
the name *Jesus* until he fell asleep. Second, they
should read aloud a certain prayer in Ryan's room
after he fell asleep each night; he wrote a copy out
for them. It spoke of faith in the Word of God, and
the safety Ryan had surrounding him as a child of
God.

Steve and Theresa had prayed similar prayers
before, with the exception, they noticed, of one line:
"We believe and confess that You will give Your
angels charge over Ryan and accompany and
defend and preserve him in all his ways."

That night they followed their friend's suggestions, and awoke the next morning astonished that they had not once been disturbed by calls from Ryan in the night. Soon their son burst into their bedroom, all smiles.

"Ryan, you slept all night long!" Steve told me he had exclaimed.

"I sure did, Dad," he replied. "I wasn't afraid after that angel came."

Steve and Theresa exchanged glances. "What angel, honey?" asked Theresa.

"The one who was here last night. Didn't you see him?"

They shook their heads.

"Oh. Well, he walked down the hall and stopped at your door and looked at you, and then he came into my room. He stood by my bed, and slid his hand under my head. And do you know what he said?"

Again they shook their heads.

"He said, 'Ryan, don't you ever be afraid again.' "

"What did he look like?" asked Steve.

"Like Jesus," he answered without hesitation. "He wore a dress and there was a light with him. It looked like the dining room curtains when the sun comes through. He lit up my room."

From that night on, Ryan has slept peacefully, secure in the assurances of his visitor, and Steve and Theresa believe that an angel ministered to their son's needs.

I have since learned of many children from a

variety of locations and backgrounds who have seen Jesus or an angel like Him. I have gathered stories of equal intensity from adults of all ages. And as I mentioned earlier, I discovered that the examples seem to fall under one of five gaps.

These are times in which we struggle between danger and safety; between direction and indecision; between helplessness and rescue; between temptation and strength; and between prayer and its fulfillment.

In each of these gaps, which we will study in the chapters that follow, I have learned over and over the truth of the slogan, "God pays all bills He authorizes." When we take chances on our own, in ministry or business or finances, we take a risk. But if God directs us to do something, He will provide the desire, the means, the tools, and the wherewithal. If necessary, He will even send a managing angel to help us through the gap.

3

PROTECTING ANGELS

All my life I have heard stories of Christians who were protected miraculously or saved from some peril by mysterious, unseen force. When I could find no practical explanation, I began to observe the gap principle at work: While God's servants stand obediently in gaps they are powerless to fill, angels protect them. The first gap, between danger and safety, is distinct from the other gaps in that these individuals know they are walking into perilous situations, yet they do so out of obedience to God.

We probably have no idea how often we have been kept safe by angels. Maybe this is because we have a wrong perception of angels, imagining them as the greeting card variety of plump, dimpled cherubs. Though angels can apparently appear in many different forms, the Scriptures depict them as powerful, fearless soldiers who take care of us in dangerous situations.

When Louis Torres, who directs a Teen Challenge Center in Philadelphia, spoke to our church congregation one Sunday morning, he confirmed that biblical perception.

A young woman named Myra, working for Teen Challenge in that rough ghetto area, was concerned for the young people who had shown interest in receiving Christian counsel. On the street just outside the Center, a group from one of the teen gangs appeared repeatedly to terrorize all who tried to enter.

For a short while each evening, Myra was alone at the Center, and it seemed that the gang chose to harass her as well, banging on the doors and calling out obscenities.

One night when the gang appeared Myra suddenly felt inspired to tell them about Jesus. Knowing the danger, she first prayed for guidance. Yes, she felt sure she had heard the Lord correctly. She opened the door and walked outside.

The gang moved around her and, keeping her voice steady, she spoke to them about Jesus.

Instead of listening to her, however, the gang shouted threats of drowning her in the nearby river. Trying to appear calm, Myra walked back through the door of the Center and shut it. They did not follow her.

The next evening they were back, once again banging on the door and threatening her life. Still believing she should try and reach out to them,

Myra breathed a prayer to Jesus, asking Him to let the angels of the Lord accompany and protect her as she obeyed Him.

She opened the doorway and was about to speak when the gang members suddenly stopped their shouting, turned to look at one another, and left silently and quickly. Myra had no idea why.

The gang did not return for several days. Then one afternoon, to the surprise of everyone, they entered the Center in an orderly and cooperative fashion.

Much later, after a relationship of trust had been built with the gang, Louis Torres asked them what had made them drop their threats against Myra and leave so peacefully that night.

One young man spoke up. "We wouldn't dare touch her after her boyfriend showed up. That dude had to be seven feet tall."

"I didn't know Myra had a boyfriend," replied Louis thoughtfully. "But at any rate, she was here alone that night."

"No, we saw him," insisted another gang member. "He was right behind her, big as life in his classy white suit."

As Louis Torres finished his story, I recognized the gap principle at work. Myra's actions fit the criteria for angelic intervention that I had drawn from the Old Testament account of Elijah: acting obediently, unselfishly, and with a desire to honor the Lord. Then, even though she appeared to be in danger, an angel stood behind her, keeping her safe.

I noticed, too, that the angels who protect us are

fully capable physically of carrying out their orders. Often those who see angels describe them as enormous beings, "big as life."

If size is any indication of power, we should never worry about their ability to protect us. Imagine this sight: "David looked up and saw the angel of the Lord standing between heaven and earth, with a drawn sword in his hand" (1 Chronicles 21:16). If angels are God's enforcers, then their weapons must be tremendous and versatile. Angels can silence the angry threats of a city gang simply by appearing . . . or divert the natural instincts of hungry lions with a word.

The story of Daniel in the lion's den is a wonderful biblical picture of God's protective angels bringing safety in times of danger.

The administrators of King Darius of Babylon were jealous of the favor shown Daniel, their fellow administrator and a Jew, and wanted to be rid of him. They tricked the king into declaring the worship of God a capital offense. Anyone disobeying the command would be thrown into the lion's den, a deep, stone-lined pit full of starved lions, which meant certain death.

Daniel knew full well what consequences he would face by continuing his prayers three times a day, but he chose to obey God regardless. And as soon as he was observed, he was arrested and thrown to the lions.

The next day when Darius hurried to the pit to see what had become of his favorite administrator, he found him alive and well. He was informed by

Daniel: "My God sent his angel, and he shut the mouths of the lions. They have not hurt me."

I don't believe that the angel wrestled with the lions physically and muzzled them. I think the Lord sent them down with the message, "Go have a word with those lions." Then the angel dropped down, touched each one on the nose and said, "Don't you touch Daniel. He's the beloved of the Lord." The angel's authority caused the lions to submit. I personally believe those starved lions would rather go hungry than disobey God's angel.

When the king saw the miraculous results of the angel's intervention, he declared that the entire kingdom would worship the God whom Daniel served. Daniel had stood in the gap between danger and safety out of obedience to God, putting his life in the Lord's hands, and had witnessed His angel at work.

Because of Daniel and the protecting angel, the entire Babylonian kingdom had the opportunity to worship God freely. Many of us forget the influence we have by standing firmly where God wants us and allowing His angels to help us. But some have discovered that help and, as a result, have brought the powerful message of salvation into dangerous situations.

While my husband was president of Southern Asia Bible College in Bangalore, India, a number of years ago, he found that many people there were open to the gospel because of the influence of one Christian man. Records dating from 1929 tell the remarkable story of the angelic assistance Sundar

Singh experienced in Tibet while standing in the gap between danger and safety.

Once when Singh was preaching about Jesus in a public marketplace, he was arrested by a guard from a nearby Buddhist monastery, who was jealous of his influence. The guard brought him on false charges before the Lama, a local magistrate known for his hatred of Christians.

Singh was tried by the Lama, sentenced to death, and dragged mercilessly to the edge of a deep well shaft. The Lama drew aside his heavy robes and pulled out a key permanently attached by a chain to his sash. Ceremoniously, he unlocked the lid and held the key until he could lock the lid shut and return it to his sash.

Strong arms lifted the lid and threw Singh down into the pit. He hit the bottom, stunned by the sickening stench of dead bodies. Then he heard the lid being secured and locked. There was no chance of his climbing out even if the lid had been unlocked. One of his arms was fractured, and besides, the walls of the well were sheer and impossible to climb.

Hours, then days passed. Just when Singh thought he could not endure another moment of his prison, he heard the key turn in the lock high above his head. Had the Lama sentenced another prisoner to death? The rusty hinge groaned, and suddenly stars shone in a dark sky overhead. Singh was startled by something rough brushing against his face. It was a rope. The end was looped, and Singh, though weak, was able to slip his leg into it and grasp it with his good arm. Slowly he was drawn up the shaft and out into the cool night. Collapsing on the ground, grateful to fill his lungs with fresh air, he looked around, but his deliverer had vanished. Painfully Singh crawled home to have his wounds tended and to sleep. In the morning, somewhat fortified, he returned to the marketplace to preach.

Within an hour he was seized once again by angry monks and carried again to the Lama for questioning.

"How did you get free?" demanded the enraged Lama. "Who stole the key to the lock? Explain before something worse happens to you."

Quietly Sundar Singh said, "It was an angel."

"You are lying," shouted the Lama. "Someone must have broken the key off my ring. It is the only one that will turn the lock." With that the Lama pulled aside his heavy robes and drew the chain from his waist. "Tell me who . . ." he was bellowing, when his voice trailed off and a disbelieving look crossed his face.

"Take this man away," he said. "Set him free."

There on the chain was the key.

Amazing? Truly the work of angels is miraculous, even unbelievable, until we remember who they work for. Nothing is impossible for God. He is fully able to keep His children safe in the midst of danger, and equip angels for their assignments. In this case the angel arrived with a rope, the power to unlock a heavy stone lid, and the strength to pull Singh out of the pit.

The angel in a more recent account not only

exhibited his authority, he appeared and spoke to
the one he was helping.

Henry Garlock of Springfield, Missouri, was
working as a missionary in Africa when he learned
that a young female co-worker had been kidnapped
by a hostile tribe. Without thought of his own
personal safety, Henry went after her, and was
captured almost immediately by the same tribe.
When he found that the tribe would release the
woman for a certain amount of money, Henry
agreed to pay it.

On the way back to the missionary compound,
however, the tribe again overtook Henry, and this
time threatened to kill him. They passed the tribal
death sentence on him and took him to their place
of execution in the jungle. But Henry spoke to them
with assurance.

"If my God is alive," he said, "He will send an
angel to deliver me." The tribesmen laughed at
him, and in response forced his head down on the
trunk of a tree, underneath the executioner's axe.

Henry sensed that the executioner had lifted the
axe, then heard him gasp. After a shuffle he heard
the native shout, "It's an angel!" The axe fell
harmlessly to the ground. Henry lifted his head and
saw the tribesmen running away. Now, where the
executioner had stood was an angel of the Lord,
shining and powerful.

"You are free to go home," the angel said. "I
have stopped the execution."

Gratefully, Henry rose and walked back to the
compound.

Henry Garlock's story shows me clearly that if we walk in the will of God, we can claim angelic protection when we are in danger, although the moment we step out of God's will, I believe we part company with angels.

Perhaps I should stress that people being helped by angels are acting in obedience to God, not setting out to follow their own wills, or—worse—to test the Lord by charging into a dangerous situation and watching to see how He will pull them out. Good intentions are not a substitute for obedience. It is too easy to rush ahead of God and bring on all sorts of difficulties. We must wait for His leading, then act obediently.

One couple who did exactly this—and who were delivered by angelic material provision—were Mr. and Mrs. Kenneth Ware, Americans living in Paris during World War II.

The Wares were horrified to hear that Jews were being taken from their homes, loaded like cattle onto trains, and transported to camps where they faced death in the gas ovens. The Wares could not have known that six million Jews would eventually lose their lives in these camps, but they believed God was leading them to help as many as they could. So they began the perilous task of secretly hiding Jews, feeding them, praying with them, and helping them escape under the cover of darkness to countries where they would be safe.

Food was rationed so strictly that at one point the Wares had no supplies left in the house and no means of replenishing their empty cupboards. They had spent what money they had, and buying on credit was impossible. Besides, they did not want to draw attention to themselves with the quantity of food they needed.

Believing God could still meet their needs, they decided to write out a shopping list in the form of a prayer. Mrs. Ware got out paper and pencil and made a list of everything she needed: meat, apples, carrots, her preferred brand of flour, and many other supplies. Then the Wares knelt together to pray.

A knock at the door brought them both to their feet.

"Who is it?" called out Mr. Ware.

"Please let me in," responded a soft, urgent voice.

Thinking someone must be in need, Mr. Ware opened the door and was surprised to see a tall man dressed in white.

"I have the items your wife ordered," he said, setting two bags down on the table.

"But there must be some mistake," responded Mr. Ware, shutting the door. He looked in wonder at his wife who was removing from the bags every item she had written on her prayer list. Everything was there, down to the brand of flour she had specified.

When they both looked up to thank the man, they realized, to their astonishment—though only seconds had passed and the door remained closed—he was gone. The stranger had left even more mysteriously than he had appeared.

Rejoicing, the Wares knew that an angel of the Lord had brought their provisions. No one else had known their needs, or would even have had that kind of supply on hand. It also taught them—and me—that angels can provide the most practical kinds of assistance for those to whom they have been sent by God, in response to godly prayer.

In every account we have examined in this chapter, the persons ministered to exhibited courage in the face of obvious danger. An angry tribe is not the safest of neighbors, after all, and a person who harbors anyone else sentenced to death is likely to receive that sentence himself.

But suppose we don't know we are in danger? We might be in what appears to be the safest of circumstances, with no reason to ask for God's help, when in fact we are helpless before an unknown danger. How will angels help us then?

4

RESCUING ANGELS

Jack and Jenny Pate looked up from their renovation work on the second floor of their Texas farmhouse just in time to see their three-year-old daughter lean too hard on the window screen. Jenny opened her mouth to call out when the screen buckled, and with a scream the helpless child slid out into thin air.

Paralyzed for a moment with horror and helplessness, both of them breathed the word, "Jesus!" It was a prayer, a gasp that cut through the terrifying realization that Peggy would land on the concrete steps beneath the window. Nearly stumbling over one another, the Pates rushed down the stairs and out the front door.

Their anguish turned to astonishment when they found Peggy sitting quietly on the bottom step. Scooping her up in her arms, Jenny wept with relief.

"Don't worry, Mommy," piped Peggy, "that big man caught me." Jack and Jenny looked around but saw no one. What man? Where had he come from? Where had he gone? There was no place out there in the open Texas countryside for anyone to hide.

It would have sounded made up except for the fact that Peggy was all right. And when they examined their daughter, they could not find one scratch or bruise. And Peggy did not seem a bit frightened from the experience.

After discussing the incredible event with other members of the family and my husband who was their pastor, Jack and Jenny were directed to Isaiah 63:9: "In all their distress he too was distressed, and the *angel* of his presence *saved* them. In his love and mercy he redeemed them; he *lifted them up* and *carried* them." God must still use angels today, they decided, just as He did in Old Testament times, to rescue His people.

Whether the angel was **Peggy's** personal guardian angel or one under commission from the throne room, they did not know. But they grasped as never before the meaning of several other verses as well: "Behold, I send an angel before thee, to keep thee in the way" (Exodus 23:20, KJV); and, "In heaven (children's) angels do always behold the face of my Father" (Matthew 18:10, KJV).

Jack and Jenny had been helpless to save their daughter. Their only hope, expressed in the one-word prayer they breathed, had been that Jesus would intervene and protect their child from critical injury, possibly death. Only He could act for them, and they instinctively entrusted their daughter to His care.

What power there is in the name of Jesus! Because Jack and Jenny had often prayed that Jesus would protect Peggy, in that time of emergency they called on His name faster than they could reason what to do. And in answer to that prayer, Jesus sent an angel.

Here is an example of a second gap situation— rescue from helplessness. If we need help and cannot help ourselves, God may send a protective angel to act on our behalf.

Jill Josten, a friend of mine, was in the hospital following the delivery of her first baby. After twenty-three hours of difficult labor, Jill was drained physically. When she stood for the first time to walk from her room to the bathroom, she felt dizzy but certain she could walk by herself. And she made the trip without assistance.

When she came out of the bathroom, however, she sensed suddenly that she had overexerted herself and was going to faint. Casting about for something to hold on to as her knees began to buckle, she saw a male nurse in the hall holding a tray of blood samples, and called out to him. No sooner had she spoken than she saw a flash of white uniform beside her and felt two strong hands under her armpits, supporting her. Then all went black.

When Jill came to she was lying on her hospital bed and the male nurse was standing over her, still holding the tray.

"I'm so glad you heard me," she said weakly.
"Thank you for catching me."

The young man shook his head. "I'm sorry. I
couldn't get there; I couldn't risk dropping all these
blood samples. And I don't think I could have
made it in time anyway. I'm just glad you got
yourself back to bed. You could have had a hard
fall on that tile floor."

When Jill told me the story later, she said,
"Betty, if that man didn't help me, it had to be an
angel. I saw the flash of white uniform and felt the
hands supporting me." She added with a smile, "I
guess I know now the meaning of that verse in
Psalm 91 about angels lifting you up in their
hands!"

Jill, like Peggy's parents, knew she was in need of
immediate physical help (though her need was not
so acute as theirs), and she was unable to do
anything about it. Her prayers for health and safety
during her hospital stay had been answered during
a gap of helplessness.

I read a similar account in the Terre Haute
(Indiana) *Tribune*, except this one involved a life-
and-death situation. Two young women were
trapped beneath an overturned car on Highway 40
that they feared was about to be engulfed in flames.
They prayed frantically.

Then a young man, driving west on Highway 40,
saw the women and sensed their danger. He quickly
stopped his car and ran over to them, not knowing
how he could help them escape. Apparently the car
would have to be lifted up so the women could

crawl out, and he was without help himself. So as he ran he prayed, "Jesus, give me strength. Help me to help."

He reached the car and with one last prayer put his hands under the bumper and lifted. Miraculously, he held the car up just long enough for the two women to be able to crawl free.

Was it simply an emergency flow of adrenalin that enabled him to lift the heavy car? That may have been the medical analysis the paper reported, but I believe unseen angels worked alongside the man, answering his prayer by helping him do what he was physically unable to accomplish. The Bible says that angels "are stronger and more powerful [than men]" (2 Peter 2:11).

There is one factor these three stories have in common: the sudden awareness of an emergency situation and the need for immediate help. There may be times we do not know an emergency exists until it is too late, as happened with Jack and Jenny Pate; or we may not have enough time to ask the Lord for help, as was the case with my friend Jill. Yet, there may be times we do not even know that some protective measure needs to be taken. What then?

Jim Arnett has learned an answer to that question. Jim and his wife are new friends of mine from Kokomo, Indiana, not far from where I was born.

He told me about a trip he and his father took to Florida. Jim, who was not a Christian at the time, was respectful of his father's faith, but did feel his reliance on God at times was a bit fanatical.

Jim and his father were driving along Interstate 75 on the Florida-Georgia state line when his father said, seemingly out of the blue, "Jim, buckle your seatbelt."

Unaccustomed to using his seatbelt, and curious at his father's tone, he asked why, but his father responded simply, "Never mind. Just *do* it." Jim buckled up and drove on.

Minutes later, Jim told me, he looked into his rear view mirror to see a semi tractor-trailer bearing down on him fast from behind. As the driver started to pull into the left lane to pass Jim's car, it became apparent he had misjudged the speed of his approach, for he did not move to the left in time. His semi struck the rear of Jim's car, knocking it like a toy across the highway and over a twenty-foot embankment.

Apparently a second tractor-trailer, trailing the first, braked and swerved to miss the accident and also ran off the road. For within seconds, Jim said, that second truck hurtled over the embankment, leapfrogged his own car, actually taking the roof off before it crashed to a stop two hundred feet away.

Jim and his father were dazed but all right, incredibly, secure within their seatbelts; and Jim told me later that he realized God had spoken to his father, saving Jim's life.

As if that experience were not enough, a second near-fatal accident only three months later introduced him to the idea that an angel must be protecting him.

He was driving a van, safely buckled into his

seatbelt, on a highway not far from his home. Directly in front of him a heavy truck was transporting steel. Behind him, visible in his rear view mirror, he watched as a flatbed truck gained on him, fully loaded with large logs. Jim told me he began to feel claustrophobic—probably in good part a result of his frightening accident on the Florida trip.

"I tried to dismiss my fears," he said, "but I was sandwiched between these two trucks and I felt uncomfortable. I would have passed the steel truck, except I was in a no-passing zone."

Suddenly Jim felt a large, heavy hand over his on the steering wheel, and he heard an inner voice order, *Pull quickly into the left lane.* For a fraction of a second he thought about the yellow line on his side that told him he was in a no-passing zone; yet at the command of the hand over his he swerved the van left.

Jim was not quite all the way into the passing lane when he heard the crash. The flatbed behind him had apparently had brake failure, and he watched, horrified, as it smashed into the truck ahead. If Jim had not been helped by that strong hand on the wheel, his light van would have been squeezed like an accordion between those two heavy trucks.

Since that experience, Jim tells me that he and his wife have both met Jesus as their Lord. They are grateful that angels ministered to Jim through the prayers of his father and others, when he had no knowledge or control of imminent, life-threatening danger.

The gap of helplessness for the Christian seems closely tied in with faith. We cannot know every perilous instance ahead of time to pray about, but we can trust to the watchcare of our heavenly Father. He does not guarantee across-the-board freedom from mishaps between here and eternity, but He does promise to lead us where He wants us, and care for us along the way.

We, in turn, must learn to hear His voice and stay within His will. Jim, unlike little Peggy's parents and my friend Jill, committed his life to Jesus Christ only when he saw firsthand the miracle-working power of God. But it is not up to us to predict the circumstances in which the Lord will intervene in the life of an unbeliever; only to trust in His ability to care for *us*.

An experience that happened to one of my brothers taught me about this kind of trust. Before any trip Marvin takes, even before turning the motor on, he prays, just as our dad prayed when we were small, that God will protect the passengers and send angels for safety on the way.

Several years ago Marvin, his wife, Sharon, and their two children were driving north of Jacksonville, Florida, when the indicator in his car showed the engine overheating. Getting out and raising the hood, he knew better than to take off the radiator cap, as steam was hissing around it. He decided to prop the hood open until the engine cooled.

But as he was lifting it up, the radiator cap suddenly blew off. The force of the pent-up steam and the scalding fluid knocked him to the ground and burned him from his waist to the top of his head.

Sharon ran to a nearby house and called an ambulance. Marvin was rushed to the nearest emergency room where a burn specialist was waiting for him. Upon examining him, the doctor exclaimed how fortunate it was that Marvin had been wearing glasses, and Marvin assured him he didn't wear glasses.

"You must have been wearing sunglasses, then," he persisted.

"But I wasn't."

The doctor shook his head. "All I know," he said at last, "is that an angel must have put his hands over your eyes. Your ears, nose, even the inside of your mouth, are all burned, but your eyes have had some kind of protective covering."

As I listened to my brother's story by telephone, recounted from his hospital bed, my heart was thankful for the preservation of Marvin's vision. But even more, I was awestruck at the Lord's faithfulness to guard His children in times of helplessness. Our entire family believed the doctor had spoken the truth about an angel shielding Marvin's eyes. This could only have been God's answer to his prayer for angelic protection. And the proof of this protection—Marvin's eyesight—left me with a better understanding of heavenly intervention in another kind of gap situation.

The Lord has directed us to pray for our needs, since protection in a hazardous world is a legitimate concern. But we must be careful to avoid the paranoia that says we have to cover every possible circumstance with prayer. Marvin prayed for safety for their trip, but he didn't mention every moving piece of the engine by name, or every intersection, or every traffic light. Our prayers should be thorough but not ridiculous.

The Lord has told us to pray, but He has also told us to trust. If we let Him lead our prayers, we will not fall into the danger of considering angels "good luck charms" whose power we have to invoke minute by minute, or face the consequences.

The Bible tells us there are millions of angels at God's command in times of crisis. What a comforting thought! And if God's children face potential trouble more than we realize, God's angels have probably protected us more often than we realize from what might have been. Sometimes we can help ourselves. Sometimes God uses another person to answer our prayers. But on the occasions when we are helpless unless He helps us, He may send angels to deliver, fight for, or minister to us.

I should not have been surprised several years back to turn on a television program and hear a prominent movie star tell how helplessness had been swept from his life and the weight of suicidal thoughts lifted because of a mysterious angelic visitor.

The actor was Mickey Rooney, and he told about the extent to which he had hit bottom. Already fighting depression, he had just starred in *Bill*, perhaps the greatest film of his career, which left him more depressed than before. Where could he go from there? Then his eighth wife left him. He felt there was no fulfillment for him anywhere; that he was a failure. As time went on, he began to lose the desire to live.

Walking into a restaurant, almost hopeless about alleviating his terrifying loneliness, he slumped into a booth and ordered a bowl of soup. He lay his head in his arms, too depressed and lonely to care about anything.

In a few moments he felt the gentle pressure of a hand on his shoulder. Supposing that the waitress had brought his soup, he lifted his head and started to lean back against the seat. When he realized the hand still rested on his shoulder, as if to get his attention, he looked up and met the gaze of a young waiter dressed in a white uniform.

"Sir, I have a message for you." The young man spoke with conviction and sincerity. "The Lord Jesus Christ asked me to tell you that He loves you very much and that you will experience great joy from Him."

Then he turned and walked away.

At once Mickey felt inexplicable contentment and peace. Waves of joy gushed through him. For the first time in a long time, he felt hope. After a moment he slipped from the booth to find the young waiter and thank him. But he found only the head waiter, who told him—to his astonishment—that no one employed by the restaurant fit the description of that young man.

Mickey walked back to his booth, filled with happiness. As he stated on the television program,

"I know I had the message delivered to me directly from Jesus by an angel."

He went on, because of that encounter, to receive Jesus as his personal Savior, and to marry a woman who shares his Christian commitment. "For the first time in my life," he says, " I know what real love is, because God is love, and we have Him in the center of our marriage and our lives."

Had God cared enough for Mickey Rooney to assign an individual angel to protect him from possible suicide? Through the godly errand of this messenger, whoever he was, Mickey's life was set in a new, hope-filled direction: from confusion and despair to a decision to follow Christ. The greatest rescue of all is the saving of a lost and helpless soul.

Had someone been praying for Mickey Rooney? Undoubtedly. What a reminder for us as Christians! How many people have been left without hope when our prayers could have made a difference? We would do well not only to pray for our own protection, but for those who need to be rescued—perhaps even by an angel—in a moment of helplessness.

5

ANGELS AND INTERCESSION

I have been aware all my life of the inestimable power of prayer, but after hearing hundreds of accounts of how God met people at their point of need, I have come to see something of the role angels play in answering these prayers. I have come to believe, for example, that when we pray, angels battle for us in an important gap, bringing answers to our prayers of intercession for believers and nonbelievers alike.

In so doing, they may act not only against whatever prevents an unsaved individual from salvation, but against whatever opposes a believer in fulfilling God's directives for his life.

It is vitally important to intercede, knowing that Jesus responds to need. The apostle Paul assured the church at Colosse that "since the day we heard about you, we have not stopped praying for you"

(Colossians 1:9); and he had such concern for his unsaved Jewish brothers that he had "great sorrow and unceasing anguish in my heart" (Romans 9:2).

If we, too, are gravitating toward the needs of others, God will endorse our work. I have been particularly impressed with two accounts of angels working in the lives of non-Christians through the intercession of Christians.

The first account involves T.J. and Maureen O'Bannon, who were living in quaint Gatlinburg, Tennessee, during the Great Depression. It was Christmastime, but the peacefulness of the snowy Christmas card scene outside their home contrasted with the inner unrest they were both experiencing.

T.J., for his part, was rebelling against oppressive economic privations by joining his brother in plundering and stealing; while Maureen, devastated by the change in her husband, pleaded with him to change his lifestyle. She would rather have him safe at home with her, she told him, than have all the money in the world. But T.J. insisted he would be a good provider for her, no matter what it took.

When he and his brother learned that the railroad office would be holding the payroll and cash receipts over the holiday, they determined to break in. As they formed their plans, Maureen prayed faithfully for her husband: "Whatever it takes, Lord, bring him to You."

The nighttime break-in went as planned. But just as his brother was securing the money in the rumble seat of their Model T Ford, T.J. heard the sound of a police siren cut through the darkness. He ran for the automobile, but saw he couldn't make it. He shouted for his brother to drive off, then fell to the ground as a bullet grazed his left cheek.

When he refused to reveal the identity of his accomplice or the whereabouts of the money, T.J. was convicted of the robbery alone and sent to prison. The money, he and his brother agreed, would remain hidden. Maureen visited him as often as she could, and prayed for him constantly.

Three Christmases later, the hard shell around T.J.'s heart began to crack. He awoke at three one morning with an overwhelming desire to make his peace with God. If only he could get to the prison chapel and pray!

"O God," he called aloud through his tears, "have mercy on me." Then he called for a guard, hoping he could convince him to take him to the chapel, despite the lateness of the hour.

A silent, bearded guard appeared, one other than the regular night guard, whom T.J. did not recognize. He seemed old for such a job—indeed, his silvery hair appeared almost radiant—but the twinkle in his silver-blue eyes distinguished him as alert and capable.

Wordlessly the guard opened the cell door and walked beside T.J. to the chapel. Once there, T.J. fell across the altar and asked Jesus to forgive him. The guard, kneeling silently alongside, put his arm around T.J.'s shoulders until T.J. was ready to return to the confinement of his cell. He was peaceful at last in the new freedom of God's forgiveness.

But before the elderly guard could reopen the cell door, they heard shouts. Two uniformed guards ran down the passage, grabbed T.J., and threw him into his cell.

"How did you get out?" they demanded through the bars. "Were you trying to escape?"

"Of course not," responded T.J. "This guard accompanied me to the chapel." But when he looked to his bearded friend for confirmation, the elderly guard had disappeared.

T.J. described him to the others as best he could remember, but neither believed him. One stated flatly that in twenty-six years in that institution he had never worked with an older, bearded guard with silver hair.

Later in the spring, when his trial was reviewed before a judge, T.J. agreed to return the money to the railroad. He was released under parole and allowed to go home. He and Maureen are now retired and living in Tuscon, Arizona. T.J. speaks at prison chapels, extends financial help to young people who want to attend Bible school, and continues to share his personal experience with an angel to help others find Jesus' forgiveness.

And all because Maureen had demonstrated one of the keys to successful intercession for salvation: She persevered. God does not force anyone to make a decision against his will, but neither does He stop dealing with a person as long as someone is persevering in prayer about him. Eventually, I believe, the person being prayed for will relinquish sinful desires in order to find the peace God has for him.

Did an angel help T. J. O'Bannon in his moment of desperation? I have no doubt: surely a ministering angel was sent to meet the need of this lost soul in response to his wife's intercession, just as the writer to the Hebrews described: "[God] makes his angels winds, his servants flames of fire" (Hebrews 1:7). Maureen had never given up hope that the Lord would act, and continued to pray for T.J.'s salvation no matter how grim the circumstances. Because of Maureen's perseverance, an angel was able to help T.J. break through the hardness of heart that would keep him from salvation.

As we endure in our own prayers, we can take courage in the fact that the angels of the Lord take up swords and fight along with us.

T.J.'s is not the first reported instance, of course, of an angel appearing to a prison inmate. The apostles in the early church were actually freed from jail through the ministrations of an angel. Luke recounts: "An angel of the Lord opened the doors of the jail and brought them out"(Acts 5:19).

A second, modern-day account that has impressed me involves the Reverend Steve Wood, pastor of the Dakota Alliance Church in Sisseton, South Dakota. Steve's parents began praying when he was young that he would know Jesus as His personal Savior and find God's direction for his life. They believed, he tells me now, that God has a "divine design" for every person.

One day during his boyhood years, he and a friend were taking a long walk, talking about the future, when they were joined by a dignified elderly gentleman. They liked him instantly, and allowed the conversation to turn to spiritual matters. He encouraged them to give their lives to Jesus early and trust Him for their future plans.

Steve and his friend were fascinated with their companion's voice and his mannerisms. Something else impressed them, too—the fact that although they were walking up a steep hill, and the boys were panting for breath, the man walked effortlessly, not appearing tired at all.

The instant Steve and his friend realized there was something supernatural about their companion, he vanished before their eyes.

The impact of their angelic visitor left quite an impression on the boys. Each dedicated his life to Christ as a result, and vowed to follow His will.

Now, as an Alliance pastor, Steve often emphasizes how important it is for parents to intercede, or stand in the gap, for their children, even though it may be someone else who brings those children to the point of decision to follow after God. That someone may even be an angel—not at all an outrageous idea if we allow the New Testament to remind us of those people who "have entertained angels without knowing it" (Hebrews 13:2).

This brings us to the second way angels may help us in the gap of intercession. Not only will they work to bring unbelievers to the point of salvation, but they will fight against whatever would keep believers from fulfilling God's directives for their lives, be it a physical or spiritual barrier.

My friend Gloria Lundstrom, whose brother-in-law leads a traveling evangelistic ministry, told me about the time angels provided her and her family with physical protection in answer to intercessory prayer.

One snowy December evening in 1984 she and her family, along with the Lowell Lundstrom evangelistic team, were en route from one town in Montana to another, believing that God was directing them to go there. They were traveling in a bus and pulling a heavy trailer loaded with sound equipment.

Snow continued to fall as Gloria's husband, Larry, drove late that night through the mountains. Just as they reached the top of a mountain pass and were proceeding slowly down the other side, they ran into freezing rain. The icy pavement made it impossible for the bus to maintain traction, and before they knew what was happening, it began to slide out of control toward the road's edge. There were no guardrails, and since they were at the very top of the pass, the narrow road dropped off into a sheer expanse on *both* sides, plunging downward for thousands of feet.

Larry struggled with the wheel, and Gloria began to whisper over and over, "O Jesus, O Jesus. We plead the blood of Jesus over this bus and over all our lives. Lord, send Your guardian angels to protect us. In the name of Jesus we pray."

While she prayed, she looked out the window and felt there was no way out; the bus was sliding toward the edge. Just when she was certain they would plunge over the side, she felt a kind of impact, as though the bus were a rolling ball that had been pushed gently back to the middle of the road. Then, when it slid to the other side of the road, Gloria felt the same sensation and was astonished to see that the bus had again somehow stayed on the road.

This went on, back and forth, until they had traveled a seemingly endless half-a-mile and Larry was finally able to stop the coach on the steep grade.

"Thank you, Jesus!" Gloria exclaimed. "Larry, park this rig until spring!"

She told me later she felt totally unnerved, and as the family and team gathered together in the front of the bus, they knew God had intervened to spare their lives.

What they did not know was that someone had been interceding on their behalf. The next night Gloria called her mother, who asked immediately, "How were the roads and weather last night?"

"Terrible," Gloria responded, and then listened spellbound as her mother continued.

"Well, the Lord woke me up last night with an urgency to pray. I began to pray and right away, just like in a dream, I saw your bus with a deep ravine on either side. I began to pray for God's protection for all of you and I saw the most amazing thing: A band of angels surrounded the bus! And do you know what? It was as if the angels were "playing" a serious game. When the bus would veer to the right edge one group would "bunt" it back onto the road. Then it would slide to the left edge and the other angels would "bunt" it back."

"But Mom, that's exactly what we felt in the bus!"

Then they rejoiced together over the Lord's goodness, Gloria told me later, and she reminded me of Psalm 34:7: "The angel of the Lord encampeth round about them that fear him, and delivereth them" (KJV). That is exactly what happened when an intercessor prayed. The prayers of Gloria's mother had been answered immediately: Angels were commissioned in that exact moment of need.

One spring not too long ago I spoke to a large, thriving congregation at Bible Center Church in Evansville, Indiana. The church not only ministered to the attending congregation, but televised the services for area viewers, and has even established churches in foreign countries. I became interested in the growth of the ministry, and found a fascinating account in the book *I Met an Angel*, written by the pastor, the Reverend A. D. Van Hoose, with Rod Spence.

When the church first began to grow, the pastor feared he would not be able to cope with the extent of the work God was doing. He doubted his abilities to handle it all. The congregation was growing; there were miracles evidenced in services; and a new construction program became necessary to accommodate the congregation's growing needs.

One day Pastor Van Hoose went into his office and locked the door. He needed to hear from God that he was indeed the man for that job. He fell on his face, and for forty grueling minutes asked God to either assure him or free him from a responsibility he felt incapable of handling.

Finally, exhausted, he felt a release. As he sat down in his desk chair, he felt another presence in the room. Mustering up courage he declared, "Reveal yourself!"

A chair placed near the end of his desk suddenly became white with light except for a tiny black dot in the center. The dot began to grow, and he heard the sound of an object moving from a great distance toward him with tremendous speed. It seemed to explode outward, and in the blink of an eye the dot had become a man—the most handsome, dynamic-looking man he had ever seen.

Pastor Van Hoose did not notice how his visitor was dressed because he couldn't take his eyes off his face with its strong, sharply chiseled features and an aura of nobility.

The angel spoke at once. "Your prayers have been heard and you are going to be used. I am sent of God to instruct you. Listen carefully to what I have to say."

The angel then talked with Pastor Van Hoose about his life and his work, explaining various developments that would occur, and making clear that he was not being released from the ministry. Instead, he would continue to be used to lift up the name of Jesus, and to help the sick and needy.

Then the light that was the angel began swirling in a reverse direction from the one in which he had come. He shrank back into a small dot that finally disappeared, whirling back with the accompanying light, leaving the pastor blinking and open-mouthed from the staggering encounter.

It was not long before the prophecies of the angel came true. Attendance at the church grew, its television stations opened; and mission opportunities came along with the finances to develop them—all without going into debt.

The message from the angel, applicable to all of us, was this: Do not fear to do what God has commissioned you to do. All of us are called to pray for the needs of others, and we should persevere until we learn the answer.

Sometimes it seems that angels are not dispatched as quickly as we would like. As in the case of interceding for someone for salvation, however, we must persevere.

A second experience involving the prophet Daniel and an angel should offer a good reminder to all of us standing in a gap of intercession for someone else. Daniel knew how to prevail in prayer, as we can see: "I, Daniel, mourned for three weeks. I ate no choice food; no meat or wine touched my lips" (Daniel 10:2).

Notice what the angel, when he finally arrived, said to Daniel: "Do not be afraid, Daniel. Since the first day that you set your mind to gain understanding and to humble yourself before your God, your words were heard, and I have come in response to them. But the prince of the Persian kingdom resisted me twenty-one days. Then Michael, one of the chief princes, came to help me, because I was detained there with the king of Persia" (verses 12–13).

The angel had left heaven with the answer on the first day Daniel prayed, and fought for three weeks to break through the barriers of the opposing forces of Satan. When he was joined in the battle by the great archangel Michael, he was freed and able to deliver the message.

Suppose Daniel had given up and stopped praying for his nation before the angel was able to fight his way through the opponents. Would the retracted prayer have meant that the angel was left without the powerful support of intercession? Would the angel have had a more difficult struggle against the powers that tried to hold him back? If Daniel had lost faith in the Lord's ability to answer, I doubt he would have heard the answer, even if the angel could have made it through the enemy's stronghold. We may never know of the prayers that might have been answered had we not given up so soon.

I wonder what God would do for our nation if all Christians would worship God—truly worship Him as Daniel did three times a day. Angels are responsible for the protection of nations, to see that neither the devil nor evil men spoil God's program; but our intercessory backing is vitally important to their role. We should learn to follow Daniel's example.

He not only hung on until the powers that resisted him were defeated, but he supplemented his determined prayer with fasting. I have found that when we deny our bodies food, the discomfort in our stomachs serves as a constant reminder of our need to pray diligently. There is no virtue in starving without faith. We could make the decision to lie down and refuse food until we died, and it would accomplish nothing. But when we combine self-denial with faith and prayer, it produces power that will propel our prayers more forcefully than before—sometimes with astonishing results.

The apostle Paul wrote, "For our struggle is not against flesh and blood, but against the rulers, against the authorities, against the powers of this dark world and against the spiritual forces of evil in the heavenly realms" (Ephesians 6:12). Satan's forces would like to defeat us, hinder our prayers, and hurt our loved ones, but *we are not powerless.* The weapons of our warfare "have divine power to demolish strongholds" (2 Corinthians 10:4). The psalmist David wrote of his own enemies, "May they be like chaff before the wind, with the angel of the Lord pursuing them" (Psalm 35:5).

We do well to ask God to give us the desire to pray until the victory is won. A stranger seeking his fortune in the California Gold Rush was said to have been found dead with this note attached to his pick: "I give up." Later, discovered just eleven feet from his body, was the richest gold strike in the history of the West. So ask God for courage and determination not to give up or give in to the forces that come against you. For we know that the angels of the Lord will go to battle to fight for our good causes when we pray, as they did for Daniel. It might even help to think of prayer as our Christian obligation.

Don't give up short of the answer. Stand in the gap of intercession, and you will find the angels of the Lord taking up swords and fighting for you.

6

MESSENGER
ANGELS

One of the first things I learned about angels is that the word itself means *courier, messenger, ambassador.* I would assume, therefore, that most of their missions involve relaying messages from God for our instruction. Does this mean that at the times we are indecisive about what God wants us to do, angels might arrive with the answer?

Such seemed to be the case with Mark Buntain who, with his wife, Huldah, have worked for twenty-six years, and are still working, to establish a church, a hospital, and an orphanage in Calcutta, India.

One summer season the monsoon rains were particularly destructive, and Mark grew afraid as flooding threatened to destroy what they had worked so long to build. The government declared Calcutta a disaster area and began evacuations.

After seeing his wife and those under his care taken to safety, Mark himself boarded a small commercial plane and slid into an aisle seat next to an empty window seat. He was glad to be sitting alone because of the grief weighing on him so heavily.

As the plane taxied and took off, Mark wondered if the years of sacrifice had been in vain. Would everything he and his wife had worked for be washed away? And what about those who had not been able to be airlifted out of the flood areas? He prayed silently for them.

His thoughts were interrupted when a well-dressed man stepped from the aisle and sat down beside him. As the stranger began to talk, he revealed uncanny insight into Mark's fears about his work in India, although Mark had neither introduced himself nor mentioned his worries. The stranger discussed the future of India and encouraged Mark not to be afraid. He even offered him practical steps for the future.

Courage welled up in Mark's heart as he began to believe that all would indeed be well, that God was protecting his ministry, and that he would continue his mission work in Calcutta.

While they were talking, a stewardess stopped by Mark's seat to take orders for refreshments. He ordered a soft drink, then turned to see if his new seatmate wanted anything. There was no one beside him.

Agitated, Mark got up and tried to find him. He looked in the restroom and into every face along either side of the aisle of the small plane. The well-dressed man was nowhere to be found. When Mark asked the stewardess if she had seen him sitting there, she said she had not; and after checking the number of passengers, she confirmed that the correct number was currently on board. The well-dressed man was not among them.

They were miles above earth. Where had the stranger come from, and where had he gone? Mark knew only that he had been visited by an angel with a special message and that he should go back to his work with confidence.

Several days later, when he returned to Calcutta, he found everything just as the gentleman had predicted and was grateful for the angel's instructions as he struggled in the gap of indecision.

Probably the most important message ever delivered was the one brought by the angel Gabriel to the virgin Mary, which placed Joseph in a terrible place of indecision in need of an answer from God.

Gabriel had been sent by God to announce to Mary that she was to give birth to Jesus, the Messiah. He greeted her with these words: "Greetings, you who are highly favored! The Lord is with you" (Luke 1:28).

The Gospel writer Luke tells us that Mary was troubled at this. Truly, it would be a shock for any young girl suddenly to have a majestic herald appear and announce God's favor! Yet verse 29 of Luke 1 says Mary was "greatly troubled" not at his presence but at his *words*. Perhaps true humility or

a heart free from pride had kept her from considering herself as one especially worthy of favor.

In any case, Gabriel put her fears at rest. "Do not
be afraid, Mary: you have found favor with God,"
he told her. "You will be with child and give birth
to a son, and you are to give him the name Jesus.
He will be great and will be called the Son of the
Most High . . ." (Luke 1:30-32).

Again we see Mary's humble nature in her
response. She did not ask why she had been chosen,
nor what it was about her that pleased the Lord.
Rather, she asked how this amazing thing was to
come about since, as she explained, she was a
virgin. The angel responded that the power of the
Most High would "overshadow" her and that she
would conceive.

Notice the difference between Mary's response
and that of Zechariah when the angel Gabriel told
him his wife would bear a child who would "make
ready a people prepared for the Lord" (Luke 1:17).
Mary's response—"How will this be?"—shows
curious and expectant faith. She did not doubt its
possibility; she simply wondered how the Lord
would bring it about.

Zechariah, on the other hand, expressed doubt
and the need for proof: "How can I be sure of this?
I am an old man and my wife is well along in
years." He did not get the kind of proof he probably
expected. The angel declared, "I am Gabriel. I
stand in the presence of God, and I have been sent
to speak to you and to tell you this good news. And
now you will be silent and not able to speak until

the day this happens, because you did not believe my words, which will come true at their proper time" (Luke 1:19-20).

When one of the Lord's hosts comes to us with a clear directive, we are well advised to believe him.

Mary accepted the word of the angel. After he left she did not boast to her friends that she had been divinely chosen, but pondered these and many other things in her heart. I am amazed at Mary's obedience, her submission to God's will, and her willingness to listen to the angel's message.

When it became evident to the townspeople that Mary was pregnant, her betrothed, Joseph, entered a terrible state of indecision. Apparently much time had already elapsed. He loved Mary, but probably found her explanation hard to believe. Should he marry her or not? What would people think? Would they accuse him of being immoral? He was in a turmoil of indecision, and in need of counsel. Finally, hoping to save her any more public humiliation, he decided to divorce Mary quietly— not the choice the Lord wanted him to make. Joseph needed redirection if he were to follow God's will.

Matthew tells us, "But after he had considered this, an angel of the Lord appeared to him in a dream and said, 'Joseph son of David, do not be afraid to take Mary home as your wife, because what is conceived in her is from the Holy Spirit' " (Matthew 1:20). After that message, Joseph never again questioned Mary's faithfulness. (The first marriage counselor was an angel!)

The angels continued to give Mary and Joseph instruction. After the birth of Jesus in Bethlehem, where Joseph had been obligated to register for the census, they learned from the Magi that the jealous king Herod was inquiring about the Child. Again Joseph needed direction, and again an angel of the Lord spoke to him in a dream, telling him to take the mother and child, flee into Egypt, and remain there until he received word that it was safe.

When wicked Herod realized that he had been outwitted, he was furious. He gave orders for all the boys in and near Bethlehem who were two years old and under to be killed, hoping that one of them would be the Christ Child. But Jesus was safe through His parents' willingness to obey God through His messenger angels.

This account of Mary and Joseph shows us as perhaps no other passage of Scripture the important role of angels as messengers, and how vital it is that we believe their messages. Because Mary and Joseph accepted what the angel said as being directly from God, they acted on it and thus preserved God's plan of salvation for the world. Had they not listened, the baby Jesus might have been one of the infants slain—in which case, would we have been lost for eternity without any way to be reconciled to God?

If angels so control the affairs of men, both now and in the future, the messages they bring us must be important, not only from our perspective of needing to know what to do, but from the larger perspective of God's will at work in the world. I am continually impressed with God's goodness and grateful for His desire to "work all things together for good" (Romans 8:28).

Elden Lawrence, a handsome Sioux Indian who lived near us in South Dakota, told me about his personal experience of receiving guidance from an angel and the good it worked in his life.

From the time he was a child, the poverty and helplessness of his people on the Indian reservation had thrown a shroud of despair over him. For escape, his family brewed a whiskey concoction in their home and spent every weekend trying to lose their misery in drunkenness. They even mixed the alcohol with orange Kool-Aid for the children.

It was little wonder Elden became an alcoholic. When as a young adult he left the reservation, he drank away his days, spent his nights in railroad cars, and ate in charity houses and soup kitchens.

One evening he was robbed and beaten by four men in a bar who left him for dead. He does not know how long he was unconscious before he was discovered and carried to a rescue mission, where an amazing thing happened. Somehow the love and caring of the people there touched a spot of longing within him, and one night he had a special dream.

He saw two frightened children, a boy and girl he did not know, crossing a railroad bridge alone. He sensed they were in danger and watched as an angel appeared to help them. Elden, understanding the angel's example, walked up to the two children, took each of them by the hand, and walked them to safety.

When he awoke he found he had undergone an internal transformation: He wanted to be free once and for all from the bondage of alcohol, and he longed for marriage and children for the first time in his life. The angel in his dream had awakened in him the desire to make the decisions about his life that God apparently wanted him to make, and to be the man God wanted him to be.

Through the prayers of the people at the mission as well as his own renewed desires, Elden's life has been miraculously turned around. He is now married to a fine musician and they have two children—the very boy and girl he dreamed of.

Elden Lawrence's experience was also unique in that he saw in his dream an angel who looked like an angel. In most of the first-person accounts I have heard, this is the exception rather than the rule. Usually the angel who delivers a message looks like an ordinary person, and it is only after the visit that the person realizes he has been ministered to in a gap experience by an angel.

There was no visible evidence that distinguished the angel who spoke with Mark Buntain in the airplane over India from any other passenger—until he disappeared. But there were any number of unusual things about the visit John Weaver had with an angel, yet at the time it all struck him as perfectly normal.

While John was pastoring a church in Bozeman, Montana, he learned that a group was being organized in the vicinity to try to disprove the virgin birth of Jesus and to discredit the Bible.

Some men in the group were ordained ministers who carried a lot of influence.

John himself had worked hard to establish a church and to uphold the truth; and his congregation had been planning to build a new worship hall. But now he feared his parishioners would suffer as the local group worked to undermine orthodox Christian teaching.

Needing time away to think and pray, John took a few days off to hunt elk in Wyoming. One morning while hunting just below the timberline, he enjoyed a beautiful sunrise on the deep snowy slopes. He was praying, asking God to remove his fear of the future and help his church raise the money they needed, when he looked up to see another hunter emerge from the timberline and begin moving toward him. Within minutes the hunter closed the distance in long, smooth strides, sat down casually on a stump and gave John a friendly greeting.

"Sure is beautiful around here, isn't it?" said John.

"It sure is. But if you think it's beautiful here, you should see where I just came from—," and he went on to describe the glories of heaven.

As the visitor talked, John had an odd feeling he knew him from someplace. And for some reason he couldn't quite explain, he found himself opening up to the stranger, explaining about his church back in Bozeman and the new group in town and even his congregation's new building project.

"How much money do you need to finish the project?"

"Twenty thousand dollars."

"Don't be afraid to take your stand for what is right," the hunter said emphatically, "and don't be fearful about the future of your ministry or your church. The money will come." Then, without another word, he rose, strode back up the hill with amazing speed, and disappeared into the trees.

Looking after him in surprise, John felt grateful that such a friendly stranger had spotted him in the wilds of Wyoming and gone out of his way to encourage him. The more he thought about it, however, the more puzzled he became. How could this hunter have known of the beauties of heaven, which almost had to be what he had been describing? And how could he have spoken with such reassuring authority about what was to happen at John's church?

Not only that, but the more John thought about it, the more he realized the man had covered the distance to and from the timberline faster than anyone on foot could have done. Still staring in the direction the man had disappeared, John noticed the most amazing thing of all: he had left no tracks in the snow!

Suddenly John's memory was jogged. It had been thirty years before, in the summer of 1953, when he left for Bible college. His old car had broken down along the way, and he thought he was stranded until he noticed a man in a brand-new car driving across a plowed field directly toward him.

As soon as he arrived, the man seemed to take charge. Somehow he knew before John had a chance to tell him that John had been considering trying to locate an old friend who lived in a city nearby. He drove John straight to his friend's house, where he was able to afford a car the friend happened to have for sale, and continue on his way to Bible school.

It was an odd experience he had never been able to explain. Now John knew that, even though his eyes had been shielded while the hunter was with him, this was the same angel of the Lord once again, sent this time to exhort him to be courageous.

His apprehension disappeared and John Weaver returned home, where all the pieces seemed to fall into place. The group of dissenters did not hamper his ability to minister, and he soon received two checks for the building project from unsolicited donors totalling twenty thousand dollars.

Knowing of these miraculous events, can we possibly believe that angels are no longer dispatched to deliver messages to God's people today?

An even more astonishing account of a messenger angel's visit, if that is possible, comes from my brother Marvin. Maybe it was the same angel who had quietly protected him when the radiator cap blew off in his face. But there was nothing secret about this second visit.

Marvin told me how discouragement had settled on him and his wife, Sharon, because of some family goals and plans they did not seem to be reaching—for either themselves or their two children. In some ways spiritually, they almost seemed to be stagnating.

One night Marvin felt particularly frustrated, not knowing just what to do. He prayed for about an hour and then went to bed, falling into a deep sleep almost immediately. Hours later he dreamed about some of his family's problems that, in the dream, were resolved amid God's rich assurances.

Whether from the dream or from the power of the Holy Spirit surrounding them, Marvin and Sharon awoke together and were amazed to see the room as bright as if it were midday. At the side of the bed stood an angel, huge and glowing. The angel leaned over and grasped both of my brother's hands in one of his large hands, saturating his body with the power of God.

Marvin told me he felt something like a strange heat, cool and yet white-hot, in his hands and burning in his chest. He felt utterly weak, overwhelmed by the indescribable power in the room. Outwardly he felt paralyzed; inwardly he felt as light as dust dancing in bright sunshine. Then he registered a mental telegram: "Fear not, little flock; for it is your Father's good pleasure to give you the kingdom" (Luke 12:32, KJV).

In another moment the angel folded Marvin's hands together and vanished, right before Marvin's eyes. The room was cast into the pitch black of night.

Marvin's eyes struggled to refocus. His breathing was labored; his chest and hands still burned with that strange, cool fire. Then life flooded back into him with a dazzling flow of energy.

Could the experience actually have been real? As

an inquiring, speculative sort of person, he wondered if the experience had just been part of his dream. But, as if in answer to his question, his spirit reacted like a cage full of fluttering doves—a resurgence that confirmed to him the reality of the visit.

It was then he remembered Sharon, who was sitting quietly beside him. He was about to confirm that she had witnessed exactly what he had, when he felt something in his hands where the angel had folded them together. He reached for a flashlight by the bed and shone the beam on the object in his hand. To his surprise, it was one of the Scripture cards from their "promise box," a little box they kept on the windowsill above the kitchen sink. Neither he nor Sharon had carried the little card upstairs, yet there it was in his hand.

Excitedly Marvin read aloud the verse on the card. It was the same one the angel had spoken to him in the thought language: "Fear not, little flock; for it is your Father's good pleasure to give you the kingdom."

Sharon was as transfixed as he was, and as convinced of the reality of their heavenly visitor. But as the days passed, both hesitated to share the experience with anyone else—until amazing things began to happen. In the following weeks they discovered a church they felt was the Lord's provision. Marvin received an unexpected promotion in his job. New opportunities in the community opened for the children. All four members of the family enjoyed new opportunities to share their faith in God, and were able to pray with people who came to them looking for answers. All of these helped to bring about the goals that Marvin and Sharon had had for their family. It had indeed been God's good pleasure to give them the Kingdom.

Perhaps not all angelic visits are as striking and overwhelming as the one my brother told me about, but the message will come across nonetheless. However God chooses to communicate, He will do so clearly and understandably. Whether by a revelation from the Holy Spirit or by a surprise visit from an angel, God will reveal the answers to our questions in the gap of indecision.

Nor does it matter whether we know that the visitor is an angel. There seem to be three kinds of angelic visits: when we sense at the time that an angel is with us; when we realize later that an angel has come; and when we never do have any idea an angel has ministered to us. With regard to this latter kind of angelic visitation, I have often wondered how many times a casual word from a stranger might have been more than that. Perhaps it was angel guiding, protecting, or relaying a message meant to encourage or point us in the right direction.

I am struck by a fascinating verse from one of the Psalms that may offer a couple of clues about messenger angels: "For thou hast made [mankind] a little lower than the angels" (Psalm 8:5, KJV). Does this mean that until we join the hosts of heaven ourselves, by the death of our physical bodies and the inheritance of our new eternal bodies, that the angels in service to God are of a little higher rank than we are? Apparently so. It may also mean they are more powerful physically, and capable of doing many things we are not, like traveling to and from the throne room of God and riding the winds of heaven.

We know from Scripture that the angels rejoice when a sinner repents (Luke 15:10), and through their obedience to God, they are actually working for the day when we believers will be in heaven and no longer "a little lower" than they. Their selflessness is an important factor in our accepting their messages when we are caught in the gap of indecision.

That selflessness is also one big difference I have found between the angels who continue to serve the Lord and those cast out of heaven because of their pride and lust for power. Those fallen angels or demons are constantly working against us and against the power of the Lord's hosts. They hope to turn us from our commitment to serve Him. We must be careful, then, that we are hearing one of God's own representatives before we follow any message, for the evil one is full of temptations.

Temptations are common to everyone. It is helpful to understand where they come from and what help we have against them.

Take comfort. Satan, or Lucifer, and one-third of the angels were cast from heaven. That leaves us with a two-thirds majority of good angels working for us!

7

ANGELS AND TEMPTATION

In our struggle to live Christian lives, we are constantly battling evil and fighting temptation. Just as Satan tempted Jesus when He walked on earth, so he tries to block our service and commitment to God. Most of the time we know right from wrong, and all too often we would rather give in to temptation than resist it.

There are two forces at work, one for us and one against us, both of which we shall look at in the course of this chapter. We also have to contend with our own sinful natures, of course, which struggle for their own way. Remember Jesus' admonition to "watch and pray so that you will not fall into temptation" (Matthew 26:41). And keep in mind the help that we as believers have at our disposal.

Fern Backer, who lived a mile down the road

from us, learned a little about this help firsthand through an encounter with a silent angel while she struggled with a severe temptation.

Years before she had battled an alcohol problem, but through the patience of a loving husband and praying friends, God performed a miracle. She was delivered from alcoholism and was living a victorious Christian life.

Then one of her sons joined the "wrong crowd." He started drinking heavily and acting destructively. Fern knew he had stolen some equipment and destroyed some more that belonged to a nearby school. When he was arrested and a trial was scheduled, it nearly broke her heart.

The day her son was to appear in court, Fern sat on the couch at home, hardly able to withstand the stress. One temptation was to fall apart emotionally. Another was to lean on her old crutch: Alcohol would surely drown her sensitivity and carry her through a difficult moment.

Fern sat for a long time with her eye on the outside door, lingering in a gap of temptation. Should she walk out that door, get into her car, and purchase a bottle?

She looked steadily ahead, then blinked hard. For a moment she thought her eyes must be playing a trick on her. It looked as if a bright light was dancing between her and that door. Out of the light a figure formed, a shape that turned into a large angel clad in white. He did not speak, but his powerful supportive presence and the look on his face let Fern know without a word that she did not need a drink, and that all would be well.

The angel left silently, the light fading to normal daylight hues. For a long time she remained motionless, absorbing the strength and courage her visitor had generated. She chose not to go out for a drink.

Her son, as it turned out, fared well in the trial, which marked the beginning of a new maturity for him. And Fern, for her part, is grateful she held firm against the temptation of alcohol, and knows she is being strengthened day by day.

When Jesus faced temptation in the Garden of Gethsemane, He prayed that the cup of suffering and death would pass Him by, but added a statement that shows His perfect obedience to God the Father: "However, not my will but thine be done" (Matthew 26:39). He was saying, in effect, "Lord, I want to go one way, but You want Me to go another. I'll go the way You want." After His prayer, an angel was dispatched from heaven to help Jesus face what seemed impossibly difficult.

Notice here that Jesus knew His Father's will when He said, "Thy will be done," and He prayed for the strength to follow it. This is a wise form for us to follow too. When we pray we should ask the Lord to reveal His will to us and then pray accordingly, act obediently, and wait patiently.

If an angel ministered to Jesus, and Jesus tells us that we will do greater things than He (see John 14:12), then we too can expect angels to help us stand firm when temptation comes.

Phil and Mavis Church faced a kind of temptation different from the physical pull of alcohol that

Fern Backer fought. Theirs was a temptation to doubt the goodness and healing power of Jesus that they believed were theirs to claim as Christians. The difficulties came with the birth of their third child.

When little Jennifer Rose was born, her parents were filled with joy and gratitude to God for entrusting them with a new little life. But their happiness soon took on an edge of fear. When she was just two days old, the doctor detected a certain abnormality in her physical responses. He ordered tests immediately, and stunned the parents by reporting "positive" results: mental retardation was likely, in addition to a number of possible physical disorders.

Test followed test in order to diagnose Jennifer's condition, and by the time she was four months old, having spent much of her short life in the hospital, her little body was sore from the probing needles. She also showed a fear of strangers.

Phil and Mavis Church clung to their belief that Jesus conquered pain and sickness by His death on the cross. But a temptation began to seep into their thoughts and conversation: the temptation to doubt that God could heal this little child, and even that He was caring properly for her. It was especially difficult to keep hoping in God's care when each day seemed to bring more symptoms and more devastating news.

At six months Jennifer was tested for cerebral palsy; then she began having violent seizures. After weeks of praying and hanging on to the thinning threads of hope, Phil and Mavis checked Jennifer into another medical center for days of specialized testing, thinking their situation could hardly get much worse.

But it did. Doctors broke the news to them one Saturday morning, when the Churches had left their two older daughters with a sitter all day, that Jennifer had a tumor on her brain that had to be removed immediately. The operation itself was risky, but without it she would certainly die. They had little choice but to consent to the operation. Surgery was scheduled for the following Tuesday morning.

Then, in what seemed an unusual move, the doctors agreed to let the parents take Jennifer home for the weekend, so the whole family could be together. "But be careful," warned one of the doctors. "One blow on the head could possibly end her life."

Heavy-hearted, Phil and Mavis barely spoke during the few hours it took to drive home. Once there, they settled Jennifer into her crib, where she was cooed to through the bars by her two sisters. Then the tired and concerned parents went into their bedroom and dropped to their knees together in prayer. The temptation to doubt that Jesus would or could heal Jennifer was almost overwhelming. But once more, resolutely, they offered themselves and their child to His care.

As they continued to pray, they heard a knock at the door. Mavis got up to answer it, with Phil intending to head into Jennifer's room to check on the girls. But through the glass storm door they both saw an unshaven old man in tattered clothes standing on the porch.

They exchanged glances. This was a stranger, after all, and how could they handle anyone else's problem right now? But sympathy must have won out for the sad look on the old man's face, because Mavis opened the door.

"Could I have something to eat, please?" he asked. "If you could give me something, I'll sweep your porch for you."

Mavis glanced at Phil, then nodded. Phil joined the old man out on the porch while Mavis went to the kitchen to fix some food. The conversation soon turned to to the foremost subject on Phil's mind— Jennifer's illness. And as Mavis came out and placed a tray with a sandwich and cold drink on the small porch table, Phil was explaining about the tumor and the operation their little one faced on Tuesday.

The old man's eyes filled with tears, the food seemingly forgotten. "May I see her?" he asked.

Phil hesitated. Besides, Jennifer was afraid of strangers. But something in the man's appeal caused Phil to nod and lead the way to the crib.

Jennifer was still the object of the doting attention of her two older sisters, but as soon as she saw the old man she smiled and reached out her hands to him. Phil started to speak, to tell the man not to lift her for fear the child's head would be bumped, but for some unknown reason he kept quiet. The old man leaned down and lifted Jennifer up gently, cradling her and talking to her softly. Then he put a wrinkled hand on her head and said, "Little angel, you will not have to have surgery, for there is no longer anything wrong with you." Then he smiled at Jennifer and put a nickel into her tiny fist.

He handed the child to her father, turned, and walked out the door.

For a moment the young parents stared at each other. Then they heard the storm door swung shut. Mavis hurried to the door and looked out. There was no sign of the man, and the sandwich remained untouched where she had put it on the table.

That night they all marveled over how peacefully Jennifer slept, and the contentment she showed all day Sunday. Only on Monday morning did Phil and Mavis feel the familiar stabs of fear, the temptation to despair.

They made the long drive to the medical center, entrusted Jennifer to the doctors, and awaited the results of the final examination and X-ray prior to surgery the following day, almost afraid to breathe.

They did not have to wait long. Soon two doctors appeared, shaking their heads and looking puzzled. "We can't explain it," said one, "but the X-rays show no sign of the tumor."

"We don't know what happened," added the second doctor, "but we would like to keep her here for a couple of days just to make sure she's all right."

In the days that followed, the doctors affirmed their new findings. They handed Jennifer once more to her parents, but this time with a smile and assurances that "she's fine."

That ride home was a celebration. Joy swelled in their hearts as Phil and Mavis each thanked God for fulfilling His promises and remaining true to His Word. And that night before they tucked each of their three healthy children into bed, Phil opened his Bible and read aloud: "Let brotherly love continue. Be not forgetful to entertain strangers: for thereby some have entertained angels unawares" (Hebrews 13:1–2, KJV).

Jennifer was indeed fine. She is now ten years old, a healthy little girl in every way. She enjoys telling her friends about her healing and she echoes her parents belief: "I met an angel of the Lord!"

As always in the gap of temptation, the responsibility for the choice is ours. Phil and Mavis could have allowed discouragement, even believing a lie about God's healing power and loving care, to rule their minds. But they chose instead with God's help to maintain their hope and faith.

We have no way of knowing what would have happened to Jennifer had they given up. But since an angel ministered to Jesus in the Garden of Gethsemane *after* He relinquished His own will (Luke 22:43), I wonder if when we choose the wrong way we hinder angels' ministry in our lives. We might be throwing roadblocks in their path by willfully surrendering to temptation.

Not that we don't get plenty of outside encouragement to surrender to temptation! There is a counter-force at work as we walk through life—the force for evil. There are not only good angels available to help us in the gap of temptation, but there are evil angels, or demons, working to influence our moral choices.

When Satan, formerly the magnificent angel Lucifer, was cast out of heaven, he took a third of the angels with him. Even though that still leaves a two-thirds majority of the Lord's angels fighting battles for us, outnumbering Satan's forces two to one, we need to heighten our awareness of the one-third that fell and of their demonic activity.

Scripture tells us clearly that these spirits have been actively fighting against God from the time they were expelled from His presence. Look at two of Satan's disguises: "Your enemy the devil prowls around like a roaring lion looking for someone to devour" (1 Peter 5:8), and, "Satan himself masquerades as an angel of light" (2 Corinthians 11:14). He and his demons lurk full of plans to tempt God's people into rebellion.

Evil spirits were depicted in classical mythology as sirens, sorceresses who sang to the sailors in their ships and lured them to their deaths on the rocky coasts. With their seductive singing, the sirens tempted the sailors, inflaming their passions, playing on their lusts and carnal appetites, until the mariners were "drugged" into submission.

The lure of sin is like a drug of drowsiness to the spirit, making us willing to overlook the consequences of our actions. The longer we continue in a sin, moreover, the harder it is to awaken from it.

Temptation, the counterfeit of goodness, comes with seductive ways and a song. If temptation did not sing or look like an angel, it would have no power to entice and beguile. Evil with its mask torn off, its ghastly deformities and ugliness naked and exposed, would cast no spell. But because we are entranced by its allure and seeming harmlessness, we let the evil ones close enough to clutch us by the throat.

How vital it is that we recognize our freedom as God's children to choose rightly! For us the sirens of sin can sing in vain. We can sail a straight course into the arms of Jesus.

I love the little chorus we sing at church based on 1 John 4:4: "Greater is he that is in you, than he that is in the world." The reason we can sing that chorus is that Jesus defeated Satan by dying on the cross and rising again. This victory enabled Jesus to say, "Take heart! I have overcome the world" (John 16:33).

Satan cannot stand before the blood of Jesus that lost him the battle. For this reason demons—and even certain people—cannot stand to hear mention of the blood of Jesus, the substance absolutely critical to our atonement from sin. Many times during temptation or fear I have spoken aloud the fact that Jesus' blood "covers" me and protects me. No demon can stand against that, no matter how hard he tries to get me to succumb.

Demons' primary focus is to keep men from the saving grace of Jesus. To do this they will deceive believers into accepting distortions of the truth. Let me show you what I mean.

An acquaintance of mine had impressed me as being a sincere and dedicated Christian. When she found out I was interested in the subject of angels, she made a point to come and tell me about her special angel, "David." As she talked, her story struck me as a bit suspicious, as though she enjoyed an ongoing intimate relationship with a spiritual being. When I asked her who this David was, I got a surprising answer.

"Oh, you know him quite well," she responded, and went on to describe the lad centuries ago who slew the giant Goliath and reigned as king over the nation of Israel. She believed David was her guardian angel and that David's son Solomon was her daughter's guardian angel, and she urged me to find a "medium" through which I, too, could receive important information from David.

This was clearly deception. God absolutely forbids His children to consult mediums or spiritists or anyone who consults the dead (Deuteronomy 18:11–12). In Israel in Old Testament times, the penalty for dealing with the occult was death. King Saul, under strong judgment from God, took his own life the day after he used the witch of Endor to conjure the spirit of Samuel.

This acquaintance of mine, far from communicating with David, as she supposed, was listening to a spirit, a counterfeit posing as David. Suffice it to say that her spiritual perception became distorted and her life a tangled mess. The voice she trusted to give her important information only led her deeper into darkness.

Another individual who became deeply involved with the spirit world exemplifies what happens when people seek the companionship of demons.

This woman I know reacted to severe family problems by withdrawing. She soon became alienated from anyone outside her own family. She trusted no one. Frantic with fear for herself and her husband and children, this woman turned (with their approval) to a "spiritual advisor" for counsel. The advisor told her not to worry; that each member of her family would now have a guardian angel for protection.

Soon these "guardian angels," actually demons, came on the scene, but rather than protect the family from supposed dangers, they filled their lives with terror. One demon, for instance, would appear as a little girl and run through the house screaming. Others took the forms of snakes and slithered into their rooms.

There seemed to be no escape. The woman even turned to drugs and alcohol to escape the reality of what had formerly seemed unreal. Even moving to another home did not drive the spirits away.

Happily for this family, they were reached with the gospel and committed their lives to Jesus. Only then did the frightening apparitions leave.

In some cases spirits do not give up so easily. They may mock and impart the message that there is no use trying to be rid of them. In these cases, a victim can speak the name of Jesus, plead Jesus' blood, and quote the Word of God, as well as be freed from these spirits through the ministry of deliverance that Jesus Himself practiced and imparted to His disciples. The evil ones cannot withstand the weapons of our warfare, which the apostle Paul talks about in 2 Corinthians 10:3–4, for those weapons "have divine power to demolish strongholds."

Demons do not attack only those involved in some kind of evil, such as consulting a spiritual medium. Someone very close to me, a dedicated Christian and prayer warrior, experienced a direct spiritual attack as Satan apparently hoped to turn him from his Christian duties.

One evening he spent hours in prayer, and decided to continue praying in the solitude of his church. He used his key to unlock the front door and after entering the church building, he locked the front door again and went into the sanctuary, closing the vestibule doors behind him.

After a long time of prayer at the altar, he heard the heavy front door open and close. He assumed that the minister, who lived next door, had seen the light, noticed the car outside, and had come to pray with him. When the sanctuary doors opened he looked up and expected to see the minister, but they were already closing with no one in sight. So he assumed the minister had peeked in, been assured that everything was fine, and slipped back out, not wishing to disturb him.

Expecting to hear the front door open and close again any second, he resumed his praying. Instead he heard footsteps approaching.

He looked around again but saw no one. Puzzled, he resumed his prayer, until he heard the footsteps for the second time, and the sound of a heavy individual seating himself on the front pew. Not to be outdone by eerie-sounding noises, my friend began to pray aloud, and then was astonished to hear the "individual" rise and to feel cold breath blowing across his face and neck. When he looked up, something grasped his throat and began to grapple with him physically, all the while permeating him with intense cold.

My friend gasped the name *Jesus*, whereupon his adversary immediately released him, as though he had received a blow, and fled from the church.

This incredible account demonstrates dramatically why it is so vital that we do not look to any source but Jesus. Angels can point us *to* the way, but only Jesus *is* the way. If God chooses to send an angel to help us, then that angel will acknowledge Jesus as the Son of God, and will give us direction absolutely in keeping with the teachings of the Bible. Don't be afraid to ask Jesus for discernment.

If one in the guise of an angel comes with direction or a message and ninety-nine percent of it sounds feasible, reject it all on account of the faulty one percent. It is interesting to note in this regard that D-Con is not all poison; it is mostly edible grain. But the small percentage of poison is strong enough to kill the vermin that eat it.

It seems, then, that we have abundant help in refusing temptation, as well as the strength to help us once the decision is made. We know that the Bible strictly forbids any involvement with the occult. We can call on the name of Jesus for protection. And His angels will fight for us and strengthen us.

8

THE RIGHT
APPROACH

It is vitally important to keep our thinking on angels in the right perspective. We need to remember two important points, which we will consider in turn: First, we are to look only to Jesus for help, and never to the angels themselves, just as the angels look only to Jesus for direction. And second, both angels and humans share a common mission—to worship only Jesus.

The apostle Peter explained that "Jesus . . . has gone into heaven and is at God's right hand—with angels, authorities and powers in submission to him" (1 Peter 3:22). Although it is permissible for us to seek angelic assistance, there is clearly only one right approach—through Jesus Christ.

When Jesus was resurrected from the dead and ascended to the throne room of the Father, He became our Intercessor. He knows our needs, prays for us day and night, and—as the 1 Peter passage makes clear—commands many regiments of ministering angels in response to our prayers. As we pray according to His will, He places our requests before the Father, then orders them into action.

Angelic forces answer our prayers upon Jesus' command, not ours. We must go through the proper channels, and we must maintain the proper attitude before God. After all, even Jesus subordinated Himself voluntarily to the Father.

When He allowed Himself to be arrested, for example, He told His disciples: "Do you think I cannot call on my Father, and he will at once put at my disposal more than twelve legions of angels?" (Matthew 26:53). So if Jesus submitted Himself in this way, we too need to submit ourselves to God and express to Him our need.

Unfortunately, we do not always follow Jesus' example. At other times, when we do make specific requests of God, we ask amiss, as James wrote, because we approach God "with wrong motives" (James 4:3).

Does asking for personal help constitute wrong motives? I don't think so. Our heavenly Father cares for us and is concerned over the most intimate details of our lives.

David Roever learned just how concerned God is. When he was in Vietnam half of his face was blown off by a grenade and he had to be transported to a hospital in the States. Before his wife could get there, she feared he might be so discouraged he would try to take his life. "Lord, preserve him until

I get there," she prayed. "Let Your angels prevent him from taking his own life."

Perhaps it was divinely inspired intuition, for she was right. While she was praying for an angel to surround and protect him, David somehow got a mirror, and felt so hopeless on seeing his reflection that he reached over to pull the tube that provided him with oxygen. When his wife arrived, however, she found him still breathing but hungry. He had mistakenly pulled the tube to his intravenous feeding.

David Roever's life since then has not been easy, of course. He had to undergo convalescence and reconstructive surgery. But his wife was at his side to support him, and they are both grateful God answered her prayer and sent an angel to intervene in what otherwise would have ended his life.

David's wife went directly to God with her request. And her request was not a selfish one. God does indeed want to help His children, right down to the smallest details.

Once when my husband took a bus ride through Bangalore, India, he watched as a native woman carrying a heavy basket on her head boarded the bus. She sat down with a furrowed brow and a frown, still carrying her burden on her head.

The driver of the bus looked in the rear view mirror and called out, "Ama"—meaning *Mother*—"set your basket on the floor and let the bus carry it for you."

She responded with a look of mixed relief and embarrassment and put her heavy bundle down.

There was no need for the woman to carry her load when the bus could carry it for her. Nor is there any need for us to take on physical or spiritual burdens that God wants to carry for us. How many times have we blocked the protection of our guardian angels—who are part of God's care for us—simply because we refused to throw our burden on Jesus? As we have been exhorted: "Cast all your anxiety on him because he cares for you" (1 Peter 5:7).

Even so, God often acts on our behalf in spite of us, just as He sometimes takes the part of loving Father toward those who are not yet His children.

I received this letter from a young woman who was brought to salvation because of angelic activity in her life:

Dear Betty,

Before I knew anything about angels, I fell backward on some ice and I felt two huge warm hands under me. I did not even hit the ice; I was just laid down gently. I saw nothing. At that time I thought I was saved, but God knew I was doubting Him and He had to get my attention. He did. Now I believe positively. I've learned about angels since then. Thank God this experience brought me to Jesus and salvation.

Your friend,
Genevieve Hanson
Spokane, Washington

Despite the compassionate or powerful ways God

can use angels in our lives, however, we need to be careful not to give credit to the angels themselves, but only to God. Angels were created to serve and worship God (Hebrews 1:6–7), not to be worshiped themselves. When the apostle John was visited by an angel on the isle of Patmos who came to reveal events to come, he was so awed he fell down to worship at the angel's feet. "Do not do it!" the angel warned him. "I am a fellow servant with you. . . . Worship God" (Revelation 22:8–9). And Paul includes angel worship as sufficient to "disqualify you for the prize" of eternal life (Colossians 2:18).

Scripture states clearly that it is wrong to worship angels, although we can respect their work as servants. They are commissioned by Jesus to provide us with courage, healing, protection, comfort, and other kinds of miraculous intervention. But angels' multiple and profound ministries always point toward Jesus, carrying His word to His people and returning the glory to Him.

Perhaps if we could keep the ministry of angels in the right perspective, rather than either sensationalizing it or else refusing to acknowledge its validity at all, the Lord would let us see even more of their activities.

Even so, He does entrust us every so often with incredible evidence. By this I mean the phenomenal photographic records of angelic appearances. Though these are ultimately unprovable, they may provide fascinating glimpses into the supernatural realm.

The first of three of these glimpses was given to me by a friend in Flasher, North Dakota. While a keen photographer friend of hers was in Italy, he shot some unusual cloud formations with the aid of a powerful lens. The picture is amazing, even shocking. In the color photograph, the sky is brilliant with amber tones and dazzling rays of yellow light. Beams shoot upward, much like the prayers ascending from the earth to the throne room that I saw during my death experience.

There are also what appear to be two rows of angels standing in horseshoe-fashion as if they are facing a throne. As they wait at attention, their arms are lifted in awesome choreography worshiping Jesus.

The photographer believes these are actual "prayer shafts" as described in Revelation: "Another angel, who had a golden censer, came and stood at the altar. He was given much incense to offer, with the prayers of all the saints, on the golden altar before the throne. The smoke of the incense, together with the prayers of the saints, went up before God from the angel's hand" (Revelation 8:3–4).

Another friend gave me an unusual photograph taken by neighbors of hers, a young couple, during their first airline flight. They were apprehensive, but their friends and relatives assured them that angels protect the airways when Christians pray. Once on board, they relaxed and enjoyed the first half-hour of the trip, watching the clouds and taking almost a full roll of film to capture their beauty. Then the captain announced they were heading into some unexpected turbulence. The plane began to lurch and drop in terrifying motions, while the couple prayed, amazed at their calm. Then they passed through it and landed safely.

Once home, they picked up the developed prints and stared unbelieving at one of the photos. There in a cloud formation was what looked like a huge angel with a confident expression and arms outstretched, as if commanding safety.

In a third example, I have a phenomenal tape recording of a small congregation in London, England, singing the familiar Gaither chorus "Alleluia." As the people repeated the song several times, they felt a divine response to their worship, as though God had accepted their praise and was pleased. Gradually, they realized, the song had grown in fullness, volume, and range: they were being accompanied by a massive choir!

After the service they replayed the tape. Recorded on it was the mysterious choir, singing in sustained tones leaving no breaks for breathing, and voices far out of human range. A music teacher found that the highest notes were two octaves above middle C, as well as the A above that, getting near the top of the piano register.

Each of these examples would invite more suspicion if the photographers or church congregation had been out to record some supernatural happening. None of them was. But how could such miraculous events possibly be captured by the human instruments of tape recorder and camera lens? I have always believed that if you can explain it, it is not a miracle. We know that, on occasion, God can and does open our spiritual eyes and ears so that we can see beyond the "normal" realities of our world. Can He not open the eye of a camera lens as well? And if He chooses, can He not allow us an early sampling of the sounds of "Home"—the voices of countless angels joined, as they will be someday, with the church's praise and worship of Jesus?

The important thing to remember for now is that in every miraculous event surrounding angels, we should focus on Jesus. They carry out His commands, give Him glory, or tell others of His comfort and love. No matter how thrilling an angelic visit may be, we are to keep our eyes on Jesus, approaching Him in prayer concerning His angels, and worshiping Him only.

9

CLOSING
THE GAP

There is much we can learn from angels, those tireless servants of God. For God has called us, too, to minister to His children in the gaps they face: to help others in their stand against evil; to encourage those facing indecision to understand God's direction and feel assured in His care; to help the helpless, hungry, poor, sick; to strengthen those fighting temptation to stay in the will of the Lord; and to intercede for the needs of others. Most important of all, we are to declare to a lost world that Jesus is Savior.

This is where angels excel. They are servants, ambassadors, agents, and interveners working to protect the eternal soul from damnation, from the everlasting gap of separation from God. In the fields outside Bethlehem they announced Jesus as the Savior of the world, and we can join the heavenly hosts in reaching the people of every nation with the Good News.

A fascinating testimony from a Japanese woman named Constance reveals how our work and that of angels can blend in an person's life to bring him or her to salvation.

Constance had accidentally fallen into a river in Tokyo and was drowning. As she struggled frantically to keep her head above water, yet began to sink below the surface for the fourth time, she knew she could not survive any longer. Then, unaccountably, she described how "strong hands" came up behind her and carried her to a shallow place along the shore. Finally able to stand, she turned, gasping and shaken, to thank her rescuer, but no one was there.

After that mysterious deliverance, Constance determined to find God. On January 1, 1954, she wrote in her diary: "This is the year I must find true God. It exists. I will find it." The next day she saw a poster inviting any who were interested to come and hear an American missionary couple. Hoping they could help with some of her questions, she attended the meeting and was amazed that they had no images of gods on the wall. The Japanese, as Constance explains, have eight million gods, everything from fish heads to hawks.

She described this new Christian faith like this: "They worshiped an invisible God who must be like the angel who had rescued me from drowning in the river—unseen. Their God was inside each one of them, and He transmitted out of them to me as they told of it, and sang about it. The missionary said, 'Jesus is the Prince of Peace, the forever joy that doesn't depend on outward circumstance.' I went forward to find Him and His peace. I said, 'My heart witnesses missionary tells truth.'"

Constance learned later that the couple had been praying for an interpreter for their meetings. Though at first they were disheartened that she was their only convert, they rejoiced to learn that she was a school teacher and eager to help them.

Constance knew her family would feel betrayed by her new beliefs and try to compel her to revert to their paganism. Sure enough, within a few days a family gathering was planned, and Constance realized her new belief—or her life—was at stake. She prayed that God would reveal Himself to her at that moment as the only God, or she could not face the difficulties ahead.

"Suddenly," she said, "I speak in English, in Japanese, then in a different language. I knew then that if the whole world say, 'He is not God,' I will know He *is* good God."

When she first arrived at the family celebration, she was unable to speak in any but the new language. Her father and brother, the "family lords," took her to a room, shut the door, and tried to "beat and kick Jesus out of me." But she felt no pain, only a holy Presence. She was ready to die for the true God; death would only mean the ecstasy of seeing Him.

The men continued the beating until her mother broke into the room and threw herself across her daughter's body to save her. Disgusted, they left, and Constance was able to escape to the missionaries' home.

Sometime after this, she read in her Bible that God's angels are "ministering spirits sent to serve those who will inherit salvation" (Hebrews 1:14). Because of an angel's service to her, rescuing her from the river, Constance had been introduced to Jesus and inherited salvation. She realized that God had been seeking her all along and had put the desire in her own heart to seek Him.

Several years later, solid in her Christian faith, Constance was thrilled to take her eighty-five-year-old mother, who had suffered a stroke, to a church meeting where she met Jesus and received Communion. She was healed in soul and body.

Through the prayers and work of two missionaries, as well as one strong angel, Constance had been saved and equipped to minister to others. She and her American husband, now missionaries to Japan, tell others the truth of the gospel, and still testify how angels protect us so that we might be saved and invest ourselves in the salvation of others around the world.

Similarly, a group of Christians in Indonesia, who were trying to reach the lost, made a discovery about the close involvement of angels. They were constructing a church building, but had only limited funds. So they decided to take a photograph of the unfinished church and send copies out with the request for money to complete the work.

When the pictures were developed, however, the

negatives were blank. Then someone remembered they had not prayed before the photo session, and suggested they try again by asking the Lord to be in charge of the picture and the request.

In the second set of pictures, to their astonishment, a tall angel could be seen standing in the door of the unfinished building, as though welcoming visitors and supporting the project.

After that, all the funds they needed showed up. And once the building was constructed, the revival fires burned and many searching hearts found the way to Jesus. The Indonesian Christians realized it must have been an angel of salvation endorsing a "soul-saving" station.

My friend Morris Plotts, himself a prayer warrior, related a third account showing the lengths to which angels will go to bring the gospel message to those in need of it, and how we ourselves can actually take something of the role of an angel. It is so miraculous that I hesitate to include it in this book. I have written it in, then taken it out again, no fewer than four times! Even though the story is hard to believe, however, I do believe my friend Morris implicitly, and have finally decided to share it with you, too. It happened to a missionary friend of his.

Ernest Bruckman had been interceding for hours at a time daily that unbelievers in Russia would come to the joyous knowledge of Jesus' saving power. Besides praying, he had sent written materials and tape recordings, all in Russian, to help those in home Bible studies to spread the gospel.

One night after prayer and fasting, Ernest looked up to see an enormous angel standing before him, who spoke these few words: "I have a mission today for you." Ernest found himself being transported faster than the wind, then walking down a path in a strange city. He passed a vegetable garden and saw a house at the end of the street. He walked to the door, quietly pushed it open, and walked into a small gathering of people huddled over a tape recorder.

They looked up with smiles as though they knew him and were glad to see him. One of the men spoke to him in English: "This is your testimony, Mr. Bruckman. We've been praying that you would come here to teach us more."

Ernest talked with them hours and hours, until he was spent. They asked questions and soaked in all of his words as though they were parched and he held their only refreshment. Finally they shared a meal with him, which consisted of a crude, hardened black bread. It left a sawdust-like residue in Ernest's mouth, so he ate slowly, holding the small loaf in his hand, not wanting to refuse their generosity.

Then without warning he felt his body being transported again. He found himself in his own home, still chewing the hard bread, with his astonished wife staring from his face to the black loaf in his hand. He related his incredible experience and put the loaf on a shelf in the open cupboard as a reminder to continue his prayers.

A few days later a friend of Ernest's came by to

see him, and noticed the bread. He recognized it as the homemade black bread he had seen being made during a previous trip to Russia. He was planning to go again, and Ernest described for him as well as he could the location, the road, the house, and the name of the group, all of which he had learned in his long hours with them. The friend promised to do his best to find them.

For weeks Ernest waited anxiously for his friend to return from his trip, although somehow he suspected he would find the group. Even so, Ernest was amazed all over again to hear his friend describe the location and people he had seen during his strange trip. His friend said the group told him of the night "the preacher" came, and the many results accomplished because of his ministry.

When my friend Morris told me this story, I had to be honest with him. "Morris, this is pretty hard to understand. Do you believe it really happened?"

He responded by reaching for his Bible. Morris is nearly eighty years old and still does mission work in Africa where he has built several churches and schools. He opened his Bible to Acts 8:26–40 and began to read aloud:

> Now an angel of the Lord said to Philip, "Go south to the road—the desert road—that goes down from Jerusalem to Gaza." So he started out, and on his way he met an Ethiopian eunuch, an important official in charge of all the treasury of Candace, queen of the Ethiopians. This man had gone to Jerusalem to worship, and on his way home was sitting in his chariot reading the book of Isaiah the prophet. The

Spirit told Philip, "Go to that chariot and stay near it."

Then Philip ran up to the chariot and heard the man reading Isaiah the prophet. "Do you understand what you are reading?" Philip asked.

"How can I," he said, "unless someone explains it to me?" So he invited Philip to come up and sit with him.

The eunuch was reading this passage of Scripture:
"He was led like a sheep to the slaughter,
and as a lamb before the shearer is silent,
so he did not open his mouth.
In his humiliation he was deprived of justice.
Who can speak of his descendants?
For his life was taken from the earth."

The eunuch asked Philip, "Tell me, please, who is the prophet talking about, himself or someone else?" Then Philip began with that very passage of Scripture and told him the good news about Jesus.

I nodded as Morris continued reading the familiar account from Acts. I, too, was beginning to understand.

As they traveled along the road, they came to some water and the eunuch said, "Look, here is water. Why shouldn't I be baptized?" And he ordered the chariot to stop. Then both Philip and the eunuch went down into the water and Philip baptized him. When they came up out of the water, the Spirit of the Lord suddenly took Philip away, and the eunuch did not see him again, but went on his way rejoicing. Philip, however, appeared at Azotus and traveled about, preaching the gospel in all the towns until he reached Caesarea.

Then Morris closed his Bible. "This story of Philip shows the Lord's diversity," he said slowly. "He can easily give a word of direction for us to follow, so that, like Philip, we can walk directly to the person in need. But, again like Philip, the Lord might miraculously transport us wherever He wants us. Philip was transported to preach. Why not this man of God who has interceded for the Russian people for so long? God works in a mysterious way."

I had to admit he was right there. God's ways are certainly beyond my limited understanding. It would be wrong for me to doubt God's abilities just because I found the miraculous hard to believe.

Yet aren't most of God's dealings hard to believe? Who can understand such a heart of forgiveness as He has? How can we begin to comprehend the love that would allow His own Son to suffer and die so that we might be able to live forever with Him? It is the same loving and compassionate heart that continues to hear our prayers and send us help, and who created the angels to minister to those who will inherit salvation.

Perhaps we question the ministry of angels because we have not experienced the same thing. In John 12:28–29, when a voice from heaven spoke to Jesus, we are told that some said it thundered while others said an angel spoke to Him. Yet John and presumably others clearly heard a voice speaking.

Since not all heard the same thing, does that invalidate the experience?

The Lord has many ways of reaching us, His ministering angels not the least. They watch over us tirelessly, helping us over gaps that at times would overcome us, pointing us always to Jesus.

Angels are watching over you and me, until the happy day they can usher us into the throne room of the mighty King—what the black poet James Weldon Johnson called "that great gettin' up morning." And there together we will worship Jesus forever.

EPILOGUE:
A LOOK AHEAD

God often does the extraordinary through the ordinary. It seems that His mysteries are revealed more fully through the simple and trusting hearts that walk with Him every day. Jesus once prayed, "I praise you, Father, Lord of heaven and earth, because you have hidden these things from the wise and learned, and revealed them to little children" (Luke 10:21). He meant in part that sometimes we know with our hearts what our minds cannot comprehend.

Jesus is seeking believers, ordinary Christians like you and me through whom He can remove fear, reveal His hope, and display a new dimension of love, especially in these troubling days when despair has settled over so many hearts.

It seems we are living in a time that parallels the events in the book of Acts, waiting for the events of the Revelation. We have witnessed Jesus among us and are commissioned to spread the good news, but we have not reached the time when Jesus returns for His own. And just as it seems our ability is accelerating to reach the far corners of the earth with the gospel, opposition to that message may be raging as never before.

Satan does not simply want to keep us from telling others about Jesus. He wants those of us who know Jesus to turn from Him. Personally, I think Satan would like to blow up the earth. That would not only kill all believers but stop the Word from reaching anyone else through them. That thought might be very frightening, considering there is enough power in the hands of men right now to destroy this planet, except for one thing—God's holy angels.

The apostle John, seeing the earth through spiritual telescopic vision, said: "I saw four angels at the four corners of the earth" (Revelation 7:1).

Now, consider what we have learned about the earth from science. The Bible does not say that the earth is square, but that there are four corners— four bulges, if you will. When astronaut Ed White and his crew photographed the earth from the vantage point of outer space, their pictures showed four distinct bulges in the earth. The first is from the north of Ireland to the North Pole; the second is from South Africa to the Antarctic; the third is from the islands of New Guinea to Japan; and the fourth is about two hundred miles west of Peru.

The angels stationed at these four corners, as I

see it, are holding back winds of destruction, the power to harm the land and the sea. Angels not only have that authority, but I believe they will someday bind Satan and cast him into the lake of fire, where he will be tormented with other deceivers forever (see Revelation 20:10).

I am anticipating that day when "the Lord himself will come down from heaven, with a loud command, with the voice of the archangel and with the trumpet call of God, and the dead in Christ will rise first. After that, we who are still alive and are left will be caught up with them in the clouds to meet the Lord in the air. And so we will be with the Lord forever" (1 Thessalonians 4:16-17).

He is counting on us to get a lot done before He comes again. It may mean walking by faith rather than by sight—but then, we have the encouragement of knowing that a great angelic host is helping us every step of the way.

Other books by the author:

My Glimpse of Eternity
Prayers That Are Answered
Super Natural Living